My Little Book of Stamps

A humorous look at stamp collecting

Conor Biggs

Published by Clink Street Publishing 2023

Copyright © 2023

Book cover design by Michael Whitehead

First edition.

The author asserts the moral right under the Copyright, Designs and Patents Act 1988 to be identified as the author of this work.

All rights reserved. No part of this publication may be reproduced, stored in a retrieval system or transmitted, in any form or by any means without the prior consent of the author, nor be otherwise circulated in any form of binding or cover other than that with which it is published and without a similar condition being imposed on the subsequent purchaser.

ISBN:
978-1-915229-27-4 - paperback
978-1-915229-28-1 - ebook

*In memory of Joseph Wylde,
savant and stamp collector*

Contents

Foreword 7

The Stamps 19

Select Bibliography 449

Citations from *Encylopedia Britannica* 450

Copyright Templates 453

Acknowledgments 464

Foreword

My Little Book of Stamps is best described in terms of what it is not: rather than being an exposé of the most beautiful stamps in my collection, it examines issues from about 400 countries, colonies and protectorates as a starting point for a discussion about the issuing country, and in particular that country's colonial legacy. The postage stamp today, apart from its use on Christmas cards and postcards, has lost most of its functional relevance, having been superseded by telephone, email and WhatsApp; its *raison d'être* is almost entirely philatelic.

It may come as a surprise to learn that the most commonly produced article in the nineteenth century was the postage stamp. As such it played a small but important part in propping up the malign colonial regimes of Great Britain, France, Portugal, Germany, the Netherlands, Belgium, Spain, Italy and Japan, as well as the proxy colonialism of the US and, following the October Revolution, the USSR. While each stamp in the book is treated to a humorous rhyming couplet, the accompanying essay takes pains to examine the context in which the stamp was issued. The essays expose the paternalistic attitude of the mother country (one thinks of the countless issues for Britain's and France's colonies, among others), the prevailing zeitgeist (Austria's love of classical music, with its numerous issues featuring composers, or Australia's love of the great outdoors), or again the papering over of contemporary injustices by means of aesthetic beauty (stamps for the Belgian Congo), or even the propagation of patent untruths, notably Columbus's so-called discovery of America (early Chilean issues feature the explorer ad nauseam). I also attempt to describe how rotten regimes, tax havens and cash-starved exchequers tend to hide behind a philatelic feast of butterflies, football, royalty and space exploration, catering for the bottomless maw of undiscriminating collectors.

The Penny Black, the world's first postage stamp, was invented by Englishman Sir Rowland Hill and from its introduction in May 1840 revolutionised postal services throughout the world. It brought about a huge increase in letter-writing, even fostering an interest in adult literacy classes. Actually, the key date is not 1840, when the Penny Black was introduced, but 1837. Before that year the charge for sending a letter was based on the number of its pages and the distance between the post office where it was posted and the town to which it was sent. Also, the sender could elect either to pay the postage upfront or to send the letter unpaid, in which case the post office would collect the payment from the addressee. Rowland Hill proposed changing this system to one in which letters were charged by weight, rather than distance, and where the fee would be the same for any destination in the land. After a lot of argument, in December 1839 the fee was set at 4d per ounce. The service was an immediate success and the volume of mail increased rapidly, so much so that, on 10 January 1840, the fee was reduced to 1d.

As a further improvement to the service, it was suggested that people could be persuaded to buy a prepaid letter sheet or prepaid envelope (the Mulready Envelope). This turned out not to be popular, possibly on account of the absurd illustration gracing the front of the envelope. Finally, in a further incentive to the prepaying of postage, the charge for an unpaid or underpaid letter was increased, in order to double the deficiency.

The colour black, it was soon realised, had not been a good choice for the new stamp: black or even red postmarks tended to be difficult to see, encouraging fraudulent re-use. As a result, the Penny Black was replaced by the Penny Red.

As luck would have it, rail travel had been inaugurated some years before; it soon became apparent that even greater efficiency could be obtained by requisitioning railway coaches for the purpose of sorting letters, greatly expediting delivery.

The new invention was taken up by Brazil and Switzerland in 1843, and other countries soon followed suit. Irishman Henry Archer invented a perforation machine in 1850; prior to that, stamps had to be cut out individually from each sheet. In a moment of foresight and in anticipation of the introduction of the postage stamp in 1840 (subject to parliamentary assent), Rowland Hill had, in 1837, also invented the technique of applying gum to the back of a stamp. Some countries, wishing to economise on cost, issued stamps without gum. Penny-pinching in the perforation department was also a feature of many Brazilian, Chinese and Vietnamese issues.

All of the stamps in my collection are postally used, meaning they have a history; they tell a story, particularly if the postmark is legible. Some postmarks are rather beautiful, enhancing the design of the stamp; others can be a source of amusement, particularly when the portrait of some pompous-looking individual is unwittingly adorned with a moustache or pimple. Mint stamps, i.e., stamps that have not been used, are more sought-after by collectors, but in my opinion they have failed their primary function.

In days gone by letters arrived with stamps bearing a postmark which often showed the town or village and the time of posting; nowadays barcodes, prepaid envelopes and plastic wrapping have rendered the postmark redundant, particularly as in many cases it is no longer possible to remove the stamp from the envelope by soaking it off.

Stamps are divided into two main categories: definitives, the bread-and–butter stamps of everyday postal needs (the British

Queen Elizabeth 'Machin' definitive set, still going strong since 1967, is a good example), and commemoratives, or pictorials, issued at regular intervals by postal authorities throughout the world (rather too regularly, in my opinion). In fact, apart from their aesthetic appeal, such commemorative stamps are nowadays not really intended for postal use at all, and many post offices discourage the queuing public from asking for them – they are available online, one is told, as special presentation packs, miniature sheets and first-day covers. Deprived of their primary function (although postal use is not forbidden), they garner an important source of revenue for impoverished exchequers; they are, in effect, a licence to print money.

Stamps were also produced that were not intended for letters at all: newspaper stamps, for instance, were once very popular, particularly in Austria, while Belgium produced scores of railway stamps, intended for parcel post. Telegraph stamps, fiscal stamps and private stamps (for use within a large organisation) are generally regarded as being outside the remit of philately proper.

Overprints are another source of interest for stamp collectors: these can indicate either regime change, such as stamps of the Gold Coast overprinted GHANA on independence, or use by the civil service, particularly in Britain and her colonies. These are generally overprinted ON HMS (i.e., On His/Her Majesty's Service) or simply SERVICE, a custom continued by Pakistan and India long after independence.

Surcharges, where a change of value is indicated, are often a reliable indication of galloping inflation, such as the billions-of-Reichsmarks surcharges on the definitive stamps of Weimar Germany, or those of several South American countries. They can also indicate that a certain stamp, being out of stock, was commandeered to do service under the guise of an altered value, usually higher. An extreme method of economising was found in certain British Pacific colonies such as Samoa, or the Channel Islands under German occupation, where arrivals of stamps from the mother country were few and far between or non-existent; here, certain stamps were simply bisected.

Keep the scissors to hand: Samoan bisect, postmarked 1895

Lastly, the dreaded CTOs, or cancelled-to-order stamps, which have pre-printed postmarks: staple philatelic fare for many sub-Saharan and communist countries. They are almost invariably intended for undiscriminating collectors, and not for postal use.

A stamp can, in certain cases, be a minor work of art, and beautiful stamps are certainly sought-after, but the highest prices paid (and they reach several million euro in certain rare cases) are not necessarily for handsome stamps. The British Guiana *1c Magenta,* long the world's most valuable stamp, is in my opinion a sorry scrawl, while the Swedish *Tre Skilling* colour error is, to the layperson, nothing to write home about. Other errors, though, are spectacular: the early US airmail stamp featuring an upside-down 'Jenny Curtis' biplane or 'Inverted Jenny' would pay off many a modest mortgage (it was hilariously depicted in an episode of *The Simpsons*). But what other hobby, I wonder, places a premium on things going wrong? Why do some collectors' hearts miss a beat on acquiring an error relating to a stamp's design, watermark or perforation size? I shall never know.

Stamps are ambassadors, often revealing a country's zeitgeist. When it comes to Great Britain, the monarch's central role in the life of the country is indicated by a portrait or silhouette of the monarch on all stamps (although there is no mention of the name of the country, since the postage stamp was a British invention —or so the spiel goes). Some countries issued stamps with a blatantly political message, such as those of communist regimes depicting glorious five-year plans, Japanese war stamps for Hong Kong overprinted with images of bombs, North Vietnamese stamps celebrating the shooting down of the umpteenth US plane, or the laughable slogans of North Korea. Stamps tell us what the issuing country wants us to believe: hence the numerous stamps celebrating the discovery of the TB bacillus by Robert Koch hide the fact that Koch's search for a cure for sleeping sickness led him to experiment with arsenic on the native population of East Africa.

Countries have their ups and downs when it comes to stamp design: Ireland's recent issues are a great improvement on those of the 1980s; Dutch and Belgian stamps had their days of glory in the interbellum years; African sub-Saharan issues, generally speaking, suffer from a lack of technical know-how; pan-Arabian issues (particularly Tunisian) are often very attractive, if a little crowded.

Early US stamps rarely please, why I cannot say, while Canada now applies colour with gusto, as if to make up for the dreariness of its earlier issues. The most consistently beautiful stamps in my opinion were issued between the wars: finely engraved stamps from Belgium, Sweden and the Netherlands — one of the few countries, along with Chile, to embrace the Art Deco style in stamp design with any success – as well as subtle monochrome issues from the Scandinavian countries, Karl Bickel's wonderfully stylised designs for Switzerland and exquisite, small-scale engraved portraits from Ireland. Nor should I forget to mention the generally very high standard of British colonial stamp design, particularly during the reigns of George V and George VI.

The practice of replacing the monarch's portrait or equally dull mythological character or allegorical group with something of actual interest dates from the end of the nineteenth century: early issues from Borneo and Indo-China in particular come to mind.

French colonial issue for Benin, guaranteed to dampen the interest of potential young collectors.

When it comes to colonialism (the birth of the postage stamp roughly coincided with the first tentative European explorations in central Africa) the British, possibly egged on by George V's interest in philately, led the world in terms of interesting design, which reached its apex during the reign of George VI (1937–52). France's colonial issues are at times sloppily designed (badly drawn, with colours that tend to fade, or content to depict allegorical figures such as 'Peace' and 'Commerce'), although some of the issues for Djibouti, French West Africa and Indo-China are very attractive. Portugal produced endless variations on a not particularly attractive depiction of Ceres, goddess of fertility (some sets having up to eighty values), while Germany largely contented itself with the Kaiser's yacht *Hohenzollern*, which tells us a lot about the Kaiser's love of sailing but nothing at all about his colonies. Many of these stamps were, of course, intended to be used on letters home, and as such projected a sort of philatelic all's-well-with-the-world atmosphere which was far removed from the plight of the colonised: tea-pickers in Ceylon, Indians shooting fish in British Guiana, a young African scaling a dangerously high palm tree in the Belgian Congo (what a plucky fellow!), the Kaiser on the Main, a native Malagasy stooping under the load of a supine colonial in a hammock. It is unlikely that the majority of the natives of any colony would have had more than a passing acquaintance with the inside of a colonial post office.

This gloomy portrait of Ceres was reproduced millions of times for Portugal and her colonies.

A glance through the index at the beginning of Stanley Gibbons's immense simplified world catalogue is enough to show us that there were far more countries, protectorates, colonies, overseas territories and dependencies than the 190-odd countries that are recognised today. Stamps from the modern colonial period (for argument's sake [roughly] from Charles X's invasion of Algeria in 1830 to Britain's handing over of Hong Kong to China in 1997) provide clues as to the genesis of a country. Examples abound: in pre-unification Germany there were separate issues for Bavaria, Oldenburg, Bremen and Württemberg, among others; issues for Annam & Tonkin and Indochina, in France's South East Asian colonies; attractive stamps issued by Newfoundland, which joined the Canadian Federation as late as 1949, and stamps for use in the Netherlands Indies, later Indonesia. Stamps tell us of countries that have long disappeared or whose borders have changed: the German city of Allenstein, now part of Poland; Silesia, formerly Polish, then Prussian, then, following the Second World War (WWII), Polish once again; the Kingdom of the Serbs, Croats and Slovenes, which also incorporated Slovenia, Montenegro and parts of Hungary, later becoming Yugoslavia; the sinister apartheid Bantustans of Bophuthatswana, Transkei and Ciskei in South Africa, represented by slickly designed stamps intended to provide a veneer of respectability; Alsace-Lorraine, part of the German Empire after the Franco-Prussian war, and Tripoli and Cyrenaica, part of Italian Libya. Other territorial ambitions charted by stamps followed on the heels of the First World War (WWI): the Romanian occupation of Hungary; the Anglo-French occupation of Togo; the short-lived but cruel regime of Gabriele d'Annunzio in Croatia; the Italian occupation of Corfu; the return by Syria to Turkey of the province of Hatay, and finally the Belgian occupation of the German-speaking cantons of Malmedy and Eupen, now part of Belgium. Military expeditions were also catered for by separate postal administrations, such as the Czechoslovak Army in Siberia (1919) or, during WWI, the Austro-Hungarian Military Post. There were also scores of post offices for the use of ex-pats: British Post Offices in Siam, Crete and Eastern Arabia, German Post Offices in China, Morocco and the Turkish Empire, French Post Offices in Zanzibar, Austro-Hungarian Post Offices in the Turkish Empire, and many others. Colombia's tortuous path to federation is documented by issues for some of its many *departamentos* (Boyacá, Antioquia and Cundinamarca, among others), which formed part of the Granadine Confederation.

The British Raj is particularly rich from the philatelic point of view: some of the 500-odd princely states such as Alwar and Bhopal produced their own stamps, while others, for example Patiala and Nabha, contented themselves with overprinting British Indian stamps with the name of the state. In Africa, many newly independent countries were content to supply contracts to their ex-coloniser: this was particularly true of France. Some of the most beautiful African stamps stem from this period, for instance early issues for newly independent Cameroon or Niger.

Post-colonial elegance, environmental concern:
Niger, 1959

Stamps can also provide a clue as to a country's economic health, such as the German 'Weimar' overprints mentioned above, or, on the other hand, the sudden increase in sophistication in Saudi stamp design following the discovery of oil. But what I find fascinating about stamps is what they *don't* tell us: the violent suppression of the Mau-Mau rebellion in post-war Kenya, where George VI looks out placidly over Lake Naivasha; the ubiquitous Kaiser's yacht, oblivious, or even approving, of the *Vernichtungsbefehl* in German South West Africa in 1904, which led to the starvation of twenty thousand of the Herero people, or even the innocuous Penny Black and 2d Blue, used on letters from famine-stricken Ireland in the 1840s.

I have tried in my little verses to gently poke fun at the salient features of a stamp or the country that issued it. If I have ruffled the feathers of national pride on occasion, it is usually in the interests of a good rhyme. As to the couplets themselves, they are intended to slay a few philatelic sacred cows; philatelic study is a borderline academic discipline, which, as we all know, can sometimes take itself too seriously.

Most of the illustrations are not to scale, enabling one to appreciate the detail of a design without having to have recourse to a magnifying glass; in one or two cases I have shown the stamp's original size, usually when it is comically small. Some postal authorities insist on the reproduction being either larger or smaller than the original, a fraud-prevention measure.

The days when a batch of letters would arrive with stamps actually affixed to the envelope are virtually gone. Gone too are afternoon deliveries and Saturday post. In days of yore – i.e., in the years following the introduction of the Penny Black – there were several deliveries a day in Central London. But nothing need prevent us from discovering or reclaiming some of the magic of stamps and stamp collecting. A second-hand album and catalogue, a magnifying glass and a large bag of kiloware (buy your stamps by weight for the best value), and you're all set.

Conor Biggs
Ottignies, Belgium, January 2021

ABU DHABI

**Derrick, camel, Abu Dhabi:
Not the place to eat wasabi.**

The largest of the seven Trucial States (q.v.), Abu Dhabi joined the United Arab Emirates (q.v.) in 1972, along with the other six Trucial States. Its enormous wealth has financed some remarkable architecture, including the Capital Gate and the Sheikh Zayed Grand Mosque.

This handsome 1964 stamp depicts Abu Dhabi old and new. Strictly no dancing, and certainly not sheikh-to-sheikh.

ADEN

**Weary monarch, wan with care,
Lovely Aden calls to prayer!**

'A nation cannot successfully govern a people it dislikes' (Reginald Hickling, Legal Adviser to the High Commissioner in Aden, 1964–67). Aden's strategic role as a coaling station (it was nicknamed 'The Coalhole of the East') disappeared with the independence of India in 1947. In 1963 it was incorporated into the Federation of South Arabia, before becoming the focus of a power struggle in Yemen between an Egyptian-backed democratic regime and the Marxist-oriented National Liberation Front.

AFGHANISTAN

**A landlocked country, hilly, sandy,
Unkind to bacon and to brandy.**

At the time that this picturesque if unorthodox stamp was issued, Britain and Russia were at loggerheads over India in what Kipling facetiously described as 'The Great Game'. Afghanistan was the proxy field of combat for this conflict, which lasted for most of the nineteenth century. Britain thought that Russia had designs on India, but it turned out that its concern was unfounded.

AITUTAKI

**World's most beautiful isle, they say;
It's not a place I'd want to stay.**

One of the Cook Islands, now administered by New Zealand, Aitutaki's first known European contact was with Captain Bligh and the crew of *HMS Bounty*, prior to the famous mutiny. It was the first of the Cook Islands to accept Christianity. In 2010 Aitutaki was nominated as the world's most beautiful island. The stubby overprint does nothing for this handsome 1917 stamp, whose frame is adorned by Māori-inspired patterns.

AJMAN

**Once mere boys, these bearded rulers
Loved beasts that purred and furs that stirred.**

The smallest of the United Arab Emirates, founded in 1816. It was ruled by Britain as one of the Trucial States (q.v.). Its Corniche Mosque is a building of great elegance.

The kitsch lettering rather detracts from the design.

ALAOUITES

**Take a moment, read this name …
You've not encountered it, that's plain.**

Under the terms of the outrageous 1916 Anglo-French stitch-up named after its perpetrators Sykes and Picot, large swathes of the Middle East previously under Ottoman control were parcelled out to Britain and France following WWI. The Alawite State, on the Syrian coast, formed part of the French mandate (the Alawi are an ethnic group within Syria, whose most famous son is Bashar Assad).

At the time of this stamp's issue a revolt against French rule had broken out.

This faded 1925 view of Damascus is set in a striking frame.

ALBANIA

Republika e Shqipërisë's **not easy to say:
Let's call it Albania and be on our way.**

The relatively poor design featured on this stamp, issued in 1945 for the newly liberated state but designed in 1943, may have been due to the turmoil caused by Mussolini's botched invasion campaign and subsequent German rule. Stamp design in the communist years was pretty horrid, but post-Hoxha has improved significantly.

ALEXANDRETTA

**No riff-raff's tolerated here,
No smutty postcards or small beer.**

The Sanjak of Alexandretta (a Sanjak was an administrative division of the Ottoman Empire) came under the purview of the French Mandate of Syria after WWI, and, owing to its majority Turkish population, became autonomous under Article 7 of the 1921 Treaty of Ankara, which ended the Franco-Turkish war. The Turkish language and culture were officially recognised. In 1938 the Sanjak of Alexandretta became the Hatay State (q.v.), which was later incorporated into Turkey. One can just make out a view of Damascus under the plethora of overprint, surcharge, toasting-iron black frame and postmark.

ALEXANDRIA

Alexandrie, Alexandrette,
Spent all my money and now I'm in debt.

Alexandria, best known for its ancient library and lighthouse, was also associated with Anthony and Cleopatra. Invaded by Napoleon in 1798 during his abortive Egyptian campaign, it was occupied by the British from 1882 to 1922. Distrustful of the parlous Ottoman postal system, many European countries set up their own post offices in places like Alexandria. This 1899 stamp, one of the 'key-type' French colonial issues, depicts an allegory of Peace and Commerce.

ALGERIA

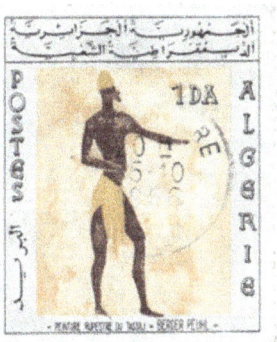

**To paint like this in one's own cave
Is sign most sure that you are brave.**

Algeria, with a large population of white settlers, was the only French colony to have *départements* (De Gaulle insisted it was part of France). French citizenship was granted to native Algerians – as long as they renounced their religion. It was first colonised in 1830 by King Charles X, who needed to distract his metropolitan subjects with a dramatic gesture. In 1867 about 300,000 Algerians died owing to land expropriation and the famine that ensued. Algeria's road to independence was particularly bloody.

This splendid stamp features a Tassili cave painting.

ALLENSTEIN

**A plebiscite decides your fate,
O Allenstein, my Valentine!**

Olsztyn (Allenstein in German) is the capital city of the Province of Warmińsko-Mazurskie in north-eastern Poland. Following WWI Allenstein was briefly returned to Germany as the result of a plebiscite.

The overprint on this stamp is more elegant than most, and rather more convincing than the heavily ornate and under-engraved GPO in Berlin, a ponderous Bismarckian pile forming the subject of the stamp itself. The building has survived, and now houses the spectacular Museum for Communication.

ALSACE

**Known for dogs and known for wine,
Less well known for stamp design.**

The loss of Alsace-Lorraine in 1871 following the Franco-Prussian War was a major blow to French national pride and was one of the factors that contributed to the outbreak of WWI. This minimalist stamp (which, although looking as if it must have been very easy to forge, reveals on closer inspection a fine mesh background) was replaced by the first issues of the newly united Germany in 1872. Note the use of the French language (except for the postmark, 'Elsass'). Since this stamp was used in all parts of German-occupied France during the Franco-Prussian War, no region is specified.

ALWAR

**This proud and independent state
Has not been in the news of late.**

The State of Alwar is now part of Rajasthan. One of the princely states founded in 1770 under the aegis of the Raj, it issued just three stamps, in 1877, all of them depicting this *katar*, or native dagger. The execution, though somewhat crude, reveals that some thought has gone into the design.

ANDORRA

**Joint suzerainty:
Oh, how dainty!**

Until 1993 Andorra was jointly ruled by Paris and the Bishop of Urgel in Spain, when, following a referendum, most of the powers of the co-princes were transferred to the General Council, which then became a national parliament elected by universal suffrage. The co-princes remain the constitutional heads of state, though this role is largely ceremonial.

This 1944 stamp is cleverly engraved, in that attention to detail is not slavish; like theatrical decor, it is not intended to be seen close up.

ANGOLA

**The brain-fever bird
Takes pains to be heard.**

The legacy of Portuguese colonialism has left many scars in Angola. However, since the ending of its lengthy civil war in 2002, Angola, thanks to large reserves of crude oil and diamonds, has prospered economically, thus bucking the trend of many ex-colonies.

Some species of the barbet, featured on this stamp, are noted for their ringing calls. Maddeningly vocal or repetitious species are sometimes called brain-fever birds. Not the ideal pet.

ANGRA

Angra do Heroísmo,
The birthplace of machismo.

Angra do Heroísmo, also called Angra, is a city in the Azores founded in 1534 by the Portuguese. This 1897 stamp features King Carlos of Portugal, whose reign was marked by industrial disturbances and republican and socialist antagonism. In 1908 he was assassinated by republicans.

A close look at the stamp reveals attractive elements in the frame, such as vines and a sort of winged cornucopia, while the portrait of the king is placed on a background of mosaic tiles. The designer was Frenchman Louis-Eugène Mouchon (1843—1914).

ANGUILLA

**I took up my quilla to write a long poem,
Got stuck in Anguilla and had to phone home.**

Anguilla was colonised in 1650 by British settlers from the nearby island of St Kitts, and thereafter remained a British territory, becoming a slave colony producing sugar and administered as part of the Leeward Islands. Many Anguillan workers migrated to the Dominican Republic during the early 1890s owing to prolonged droughts.

In common with many issues of the Caribbean islands, Anguilla's modern stamp design is disappointing.

ANJOUAN

**Comoro Isles, near Madagascar?
She kissed me any time I asked her.**

Anjouan is one of the four Comoros Islands. In 1843 France officially took possession of Mayotte, and in 1886 it placed the other three islands under its protection. Administratively attached to Madagascar in 1912, Comoros became an overseas territory of France in 1947 and was given representation in the French National Assembly. Its modern name is Ndzuwani.

This 'Peace and Commerce' stamp, issued in 1892, was transported wholesale from metropolitan France. It is greatly improved by the attractive postmark.

ANNAM & TONKIN

**Annam & Tonkin, a husband & wife,
Exhibited tokens of marital strife.**

Annam was a French protectorate encompassing Central Vietnam, later becoming a part of French Indo-China. New colonies such as Annam & Tonkin were expected to be self-financing; this was achieved through forced labour, a hut tax and conscription into the French army in time of war.

This is a 'Mouchon' key-type stamp named after its designer. The squat surcharge is the philatelic equivalent of going to bed with muddy boots.

ANTIGUA

**What, Windsor Castle in Antigua?
If you ask me, that's ambigua.**

One of the Lesser Antilles, Antigua was visited in 1493 by Christopher Columbus, who named it for the Church of Santa Maria de la Antigua in Seville. It was colonised by English settlers in 1632. Like so many of its neighbours, it was a slave colony producing sugar and human misery.

This stamp was one of a British Empire-wide issue marking the Silver Jubilee of George V in 1935. There is a great deal of lavish detail to enjoy, but one is left in no doubt as to the centre of power: Merrie Windsor.

ANTIOQUIA

**Antioquia, now, is much overrated,
And what is worse still, quite antioquated.**

The Colombian department of Antioquia was formerly one of the thirty-two states of the Granadine Confederation which now make up modern-day Colombia. The influence of the Basque language can still be felt in Antioquia, owing to the arrival of Basques there in 1499, during Columbus's third voyage. Many Basques also fled there following the Spanish Civil War. Its stamp design, in common with most of South America's early issues, is deadly dull. What, I wonder, is the point of surrounding such an ugly numeral with a pretty, floral pattern?

ARBE

**But who's this on the outside rail?
It's Arbe! Arbe's won the Derby!**

An island in the Adriatic Sea in western Croatia now known as Rab, Arbe was invaded by the poet and fascist demagogue Gabriele D'Annunzio in 1919, becoming part of the Regency of Carnaro. D'Annunzio, who was renowned for his military exploits, was unhappy that Fiume was to be ceded to the Kingdom of the Serbs, Croats and Slovenes, created under the terms of the Treaty of Versailles. His brutal tactics were much admired by Mussolini; in fact, he could be said to be one of the founding fathers of Italian fascism. His short-lived regency was ended by the intervention of the Italian military in 1920.

ARGENTINA

**Buenos Dias, Argentina!
(Can't say that I've ever beena.)**

The high-value denominations of the 1936 'Patriots and Natural Resources' issue unsurprisingly show a selection of the country's natural resources, such as wool production and oil. This beautifully engraved stamp features a Patagonian ram.

Argentina under President Hipólito Yrigoyen saw the suppression of the 1921 Patagonian sheepherders' strike, when 300 strikers were shot or executed.

ARMENIA

**Best alphabet I've ever seen,
In red and yellow, blue & green.**

If you have it, flaunt it – the Armenian alphabet is surely one of the most beautiful. The *Encyclopaedia Britannica* tells us that 'the invention of the Armenian alphabet is traditionally credited to the monk St. Mesrop Mashtots, who in AD 405 created an alphabet consisting of thirty-six signs (two were added later) based partly on Greek letters; the direction of writing (left to right) also followed the Greek model. This new alphabet was first used to translate the Hebrew Bible and the Christian New Testament.'

This stamp is one of a set issued in 2013.

ASCENSION

**Ascension Island, rather lonely,
But those Three Sisters – oh, how homely!**

Ascension is a volcanic island in the South Atlantic Ocean, part of the British Overseas Territory of St Helena, Ascension and Tristan da Cunha. It was named for the day on which it was discovered in 1501 by João da Nova. British marines were stationed there during the exile of Napoleon on St Helena, in order to discourage French incursions.

In 1934 a pictorial series of ten engraved stamps was issued, depicting various views of the island. In 1938 these stamps, in common with many other British colonies, were re-issued with a portrait of George VI, setting a benchmark for colonial stamp design.

AUSTRALIA

**A hop, a skip, and – *inter alia* –
You'll find yerself, mate, in Australia.**

Australian philately proper begins with its first issue in 1913, twelve years after federation: these are the famous 'Roo' stamps, which are highly sought-after, no doubt on account of their strikingly simple design. They were the first stamps to feature the new country's name. The reason for the delay in issuing them was political: there was considerable opposition to the inclusion of royal symbols or profiles.

This attractive stamp is one of a set of twenty issued in 1937.

AUSTRIA

„Briefmarke: © Österreichische Post Ag"

**Mozart, Haydn, flippin' Strauss,
Not the place for shootin' grouse.**

I have never warmed to Austrian stamps – the spirit of those pesky putti in over-coloured rococo churches is omnipresent. Exceptions are the 1948 Provincial Costumes set and the beautiful Koloman Moser issues of 1906, marking the sixtieth anniversary of the accession of Franz Joseph, who features on this early stamp. Note the absence of the country name, and the emperor's Vercingetorix look.

AUSTRIAN TERRITORIES ACQUIRED BY ITALY

„*Briefmarke: © Österreichische Post Ag*"

Backed the loser, never mind:
That's what happens to mankind.

In the world of philately, when power changes hands, the overprint machine is cranked up. Austria was forced to relinquish some of its territory in the Tyrol to Italy following WWI; this stamp, in use for about two years, was originally Austrian. To the victor the spoils, although the overprint *(Regno d'Italia Trentino 3 nov. 1918)* is discreet to the point of being difficult to read.

AUSTRO-HUNGARIAN MILITARY POST

„Briefmarke: © Österreichische Post Ag"

**Bearded worthy, rather smug,
Love to give his beard a tug.**

During WWI, Austria issued stamps for its troops in Italy, Bosnia, Montenegro, Romania and Serbia. *K.u.K.* stands for *Kaiserliche und Königliche,* or 'Imperial and Royal'.

A dyspeptic Franz Joseph is treated to a very handsome 'metalwork' frame, a feature of Secession-inspired stamp design.

AUSTRO-HUNGARIAN POST OFFICES IN THE TURKISH EMPIRE

„Briefmarke: © Österreichische Post Ag"

**Francis Joseph's sticking plaster
Came unstuck, cost one piastre.**

Motivated by the poor postal service in the Ottoman Empire, several European countries, including Austria, opened their own post offices. In 1721 the Ottoman Empire gave Austria permission to operate a postal service for official correspondence only.

More dyspeptic emperor, this time in profile, complete with Latin inscription.

AZERBAIJAN

**Turtles I saw in Azerbaijan,
Lumbering beasties to a man.**

Azerbaijan's most interesting stamps were issued during its short pre-Soviet independence, from 1919 to 1920, with some stragglers in 1921, including a harrowing set entitled 'Famine Relief'. Later issues, like the one illustrated above, are generally uninspiring; this 1995 stamp has been cancelled to order (i.e., it was not used postally) and was intended to be sold to foreign collectors as a source of extra revenue.

AZORES

**If I'd a girlfriend called Dolores,
I'd take her post-haste to th'Azores.**

Many of the Azores' early settlers were Portuguese Sephardic Jews who were exiled there by the Portuguese Inquisition. Later settlers included the Flemish, whose numbers caused the islands to be nicknamed 'The Isles of Flanders'. The earliest issues for the archipelago were Portuguese; the first Azores stamps date from 1868 and were in use until 1930, after which Portuguese stamps were used once more. This stamp, a 'key-type', depicting a well-fed Ceres, goddess of the regenerative power of nature, comes from a set of ninety-one identical stamps. Later issues are more interesting, I promise.

BADEN

**A man named Aidan went to Baden.
I don't know Howell, he's now called Powell.**

On 1 May 1851 The Grand Duchy of Baden joined the German-Austrian Postal Union. On the same day, Baden's first stamps were issued; this one dates from 1862.

Baden's '9 Kreuzer Green' is one of the great philatelic rarities: green paper, intended for the 6 Kreuzer value, was used instead to print a number of 9 Kreuzer stamps (the mistake is understandable, since an upside-down '6' resembles a '9' and vice versa).

In common with many other stamps issued by the individual German states, this 1860 stamp is square in shape. And rather dull to boot.

BAGHDAD

**Tigris, Euphrates, Mesopotamia,
Hats off to this *metropolania!***

This 1913 Turkish stamp predates Britain's 1917 invasion of Baghdad on the grounds that the Turkish presence there threatened the Allied cause (in fact, it was probably because of Britain's vested interest in the recently established Turkish Petroleum Company). It depicts the Lighthouse Garden in Constantinople and bears the words POSTES OTTOMANES, presumably for the benefit of French settlers. The poorly executed overprint, dating from the British invasion, rather spoils an attractive stamp.

BAHAMAS

**I know this bloke, he likes a smoke,
Never gets up, stays in pyjamas.**

Good design is all about avoiding clutter: this is a lovely example, a portrait of Edward VII issued in 1902. There are few pictorial stamps dating from his reign, which of course simplified matters for the designer. But the detail of the frame, incorporating local flora, is charming.

Before I die I should like to taste a Bahamian national dish, Guava Duff, a mixture of boiled fruit and dough that is served with a butter sauce.

BAHAWALPUR

**H. H. th'Amir of Bahawalpur,
A talented arboreal planter.**

A former feudatory state of India under British rule, Bahawalpur became part of Pakistan in 1947. From 1947 until 1949 it issued its own rather attractive stamps, which continued to be used until 1953. This 1949 issue features Sir Sadeq Muhammad Khan Abbasi, H. H. the Amir of Bahawalpur, who ceded Bahawalpur to Pakistan following Indian independence, making it the second of fourteen Indian feudatory states to become part of the new country.

BAHRAIN

**I know this guy, he loves the rain,
He says he doesn't miss Bahrain.**

Under the terms of a treaty signed by Britain and Bahrain in 1861, war, piracy and slavery were forbidden in Bahrain, in return for which Britain undertook to defend it if necessary. Bahrain (which is a little bigger than Singapore) became independent in 1971, following Britain's decision to withdraw all its forces from the Gulf in 1968. British Indian stamps overprinted BAHRAIN were used from 1933 to 1947, presumably to cut costs: the same approach was adopted for Indian stamps overprinted BURMA. Here, the 'Indian' features are somewhat overdone.

BAMRA

**Bamra … Bamra …
Where I lost my camra.**

Bamra State was one of the princely (feudatory) states of India during the period of the Raj, becoming part of India in 1948. In 1888 and 1890 it issued a handful of stamps that look as if they might have been cinema stubs. The uninspiring little drawing in the centre of this stamp depicts an elephant's trunk holding a stick.

BARBADOS

**The weather forecast for Barbados:
Scattered showers and tornados.**

One of the sugar islands, modern-day Barbados is considered to be one of the more successful democracies in the West Indies. The elegant 'Inter Colonial Schooner' depicted on this early QEII stamp, issued in 1953, is graced with a full-blooded postmark.

The territories of the West Indies under British rule were initially cut off from each other: for example, letters from Jamaica to Barbados had to go via Halifax, New York or London. So much for inter-colonial.

BASUTOLAND

**A king, a crocodile, high mountains:
No bosky glades or glittering fountains.**

In the 1820s the various tribes that had settled in Basutoland were consolidated into the Kingdom of Sotho under King Moshoeshoe I. Disputes with the Boers led the king to appeal to Britain for help, which subsequently granted protectorate status to Basutoland. Fears that Britain should cede the country to South Africa proved unfounded, and so this small mountainous kingdom remained more or less intact until independence (as Lesotho).

The stamp is a delightful flight of fantasy.

BATUM

**The other day in downtown Batum
I bought two pounds of fresh tomatum.**

Batumi (or Batum) is a city on the Black Sea in Georgia. In 1918 the Treaty of Brest-Litovsk returned the city to the Ottoman Empire, but civil unrest followed, and in December 1918 the city was taken by British forces, who remained until 1920. This 1919 stamp depicts a lacklustre aloe tree, mostly obscured by the shabbily executed overprint and postmark. Numerous forgeries exist – have I been duped? The poor paper quality does nothing for the overall impression.

BAVARIA

**I had a beer once in Bavaria,
And lo! I came down with malaria.**

Bavaria, although integrated into the newly united Germany in 1871, retained much of its independence – and its royal family – until 1918. Ludwig II, of Schloss Neuschwanstein fame, was declared insane in 1886 (he may simply have been very eccentric) and was replaced by his uncle Luitpold, the twenty-fifth anniversary of whose regency is celebrated in this ghastly stamp.

BECHUANALAND PROTECTORATE

King George's Silver Jubilee
Had little consequence for me.

White miners and gold prospectors flooded into what is now Botswana in 1867–69 to start a short-lived mining rush. The Protectorate's original *raison d'être* was to thwart German expansion and, above all, to prevent an alliance between Germany and the Boer Republic of Transvaal. Bechuanaland was useful only insofar as it provided the means to build a rail link between South Africa and Rhodesia. Attempts to cede it to either Rhodesia or South Africa failed, leading to independence as Botswana in 1966.

BELARUS

**I'm dreaming of a White Russian,
Just like the one I used to know.**

At various times occupied by Poland, Lithuania and Russia, Belarus saw much of its population emigrate in the years before the Russian Revolution, owing to economic hardship. Independent since 1991, Belarus issues cheerfully undistinguished stamps, curious given the beauty of its national flag. This one depicts the *kryzhachok,* a folk dance.

BELGIAN CONGO

©Bpost

**Choo-choo, tiny little train,
Do your best to hide the pain.**

All colonial powers displayed paternalism: it was part of the *mission civilisatrice* which lasted in the case of Congo until independence in 1960. But few colonial powers committed as many atrocities as the Belgian concessionary companies in the Congo in their quest for rubber.

This stamp was issued for Leopold II's private domain, the Independent State of Congo. The frame is extraordinarily elaborate, calling to mind the design for a banknote. The vignette is based on a diorama.

BELGIAN OCCUPATION OF GERMANY

©Bpost

**Wartime reparation
Can sometimes heal a nation.**

The Treaty of Versailles (1919) stipulated that Germany hand over a small portion of its western territory to Belgium by way of war reparation. The Belgian East Cantons now form an autonomous German-speaking region with their own parliament. This 'Liberation' stamp features the *Perron* at Liège, a fountain constructed in 1305, representing that city's freedom; it is also its symbol. Note the bilingual overprint, with the old Dutch spelling of 'Duitschland', now simply spelt 'Duitsland'. The frame suggests Art Nouveau influence.

BELGIUM

©*Bpost*

**Buffer state between two powers,
Lace, canals and nice bell-towers.**

Constitutionally a total maze (it has six parliaments), Belgium is a fascinating country whose charms lie hidden deep beneath its surface. Never mind its chocolate and beer; its contribution to art and music in the heyday of the Flemish-Burgundian Empire is a source of great national pride. The occasional linguistic tiffs cannot hide the fact that, as cobbled-together nations go, Belgium is a success.

Note the detachable label at the bottom of the stamp: if the sender did not remove it, the letter was not delivered on Sunday, a unique and humane gesture.

BENIN

**In case you were wondering, Lenin
Was not born in far-distant Benin.**

Another key-type stamp, and, in common with French colonial issues of the period, blithely indifferent to the culture of Benin, or Dahomey, as it was then known. The Republic of Dahomey was renamed the People's Republic of Benin in 1975. No fewer than six military coups have taken place between 1963 and 1972; recently, it has become more stable but remains one of the world's poorest countries. Note the GOLFE DE BÉNIN (Bight of Benin), from which the country takes its name, simply inserted into a one-purpose-suits-all-colonies tablet at the base of the stamp. Later issues, in common with those of most of sub-Saharan Africa, are disappointing.

BERMUDA

**Birds & bees & fragrant bowers,
Winter winds & summer showers.**

Bermuda was named after Juan Bermúdez, possibly as early as 1503. In 1609 the *Sea Venture,* en route to Virginia, was blown off course by a hurricane and shipwrecked off Bermuda. Shakespeare's *The Tempest* was inspired by the event: Ariel makes reference to 'the still-vex'd Bermoothes'.

This 1936 stamp, a view of a house at Par-la-Ville, Hamilton, uses a daring colour combination. It breathes an air of Agatha Christie.

BHOPAL

**Central Indian state of yore,
Righteous to its very core.**

Bhopal, the capital of Madhya Pradesh in Central India, was on friendly terms with the Raj. In 1984 it became famous for the worst industrial accident in history.

Compared to some other Indian states, such as Charkhari (q.v.) or Bhor (q.v.), Bhopal's stamp designs were quite stylish. Note the quality of the paper.

BHOR

**I wintered in Bhor,
And came back for mhore.**

Bhor is a town in the state of Maharashtra, India, situated in the Western Ghats. Like many Indian feudatory states under the Raj it had its own postal administration, which was presumably responsible for this hideous stamp, issued in 1879. Collectors refer to such stamps as 'Uglies'.

BHUTAN

**Mountain state, no palmy beaches:
Steep inclines and giant leeches.**

Some of Bhutan's stamps have been relegated to what the Stanley Gibbons catalogue refers to as the *Appendix,* generally meaning stamps 'issued in excess of postal needs or … not available to the public in reasonable quantities at face value'. Come to think of it, this is often now the case in all but the biggest of Europe's post offices: in smaller branches, commemorative issues need to be ordered beforehand, or online.

This 1968 stamp depicts Tongsa (now Trongsa) Dzong, the largest dzong (fortress) in Bhutan.

BIAFRA

**Biafranisation
Takes organisation.**

Biafra seceded from Nigeria in 1967. The secession was led by the Igbo people and gave rise to the Nigerian-Biafran War, ending in 1970. I remember as a child being told to think of starving Biafran children when unwilling to finish my dinner.

The Biafran war was a legacy of British colonialism. Hardly anywhere else in Africa was the imposition of arbitrary political boundaries for the purposes of administrative convenience to have such a pernicious effect.

BIJAWAR

**This bearded bloke in sumptuous headdress
When asked in marriage stuttered 'yesyes'.**

Bijawar was one of the Indian feudatory states, now part of the state of Madhya Pradesh. It was rewarded for supporting the British in the 1857 Mutiny by, among other things, a hereditary salute of eleven guns (the trappings of royalty were greatly appreciated by local Indian rulers).

This 1935 stamp depicts the Maharaj Sarwant Singh in attractive homespun guise.

BOHEMIA & MORAVIA

**Bohemia, Moravia,
Armenia, Belgravia.**

Following Slovakia's declaration of independence in 1939, the Czech provinces of Bohemia and Moravia became a German Protectorate from 1939 to 1945. Its issues were remarkably similar to some of the first Czechoslovakian ones, which is to say well designed if a little dull. This attractive stamp features the railway bridge at Bechyně (Beching).

BOLIVIA

**I can't find a rhyme for Bolivia!
Ideas, my dearest Olivia?**

This 1960 stamp celebrates the Bolivian violinist Jaime Laredo, known for his incandescent tone. That same year saw the issue of another set designed in *1926* to commemorate Bolivian independence, which had been printed in Germany and sold (without permission) to collectors. The Bolivian postal authorities angrily ordered the remainder to be locked in a bank vault for thirty-five years. Unfortunately, chronic inflation had caught up with these philatelic Rip Van Winkles, which meant that when they were finally released from captivity, they required surcharging of up to 10,000 times their original value.

BOPHUTHATSWANA

**'I name this child Bophuthatswana',
Intoned the vicar. Poof! Nirvana.**

The South African Bantustans were apartheid enclaves in which citizens were stripped of their South African citizenship and forbidden to leave. Not surprisingly, the Bantustans remained underdeveloped and impoverished. Bophuthatswana, one of ten South African Bantustans, was created in 1977 and reincorporated into post-apartheid South Africa in 1994.

This rather grim 1979 stamp is a remarkable piece of anti-smoking propaganda.

BOSNIA & HERZEGOVINA

**Town of very sad repute:
Sarajevo, branch and root.**

This lovely 1906 depiction of St Luke's campanile in Jajce, surrounded by a floral design, betrays the influence of the Viennese Secessionist Movement and its close relative, the Arts and Crafts Movement in Great Britain. It was designed by Koloman Moser, who also designed certain Austrian stamps of the same period. One of the loveliest sets ever issued.

BOTSWANA

**Formerly Bechuanaland,
Botswana now: birds, bees and sand.**

The name Botswana derives from the 'Tswana', the country's dominant ethnic group (also known as the 'Bechuana', hence the pre-independence name, Bechuanaland [q.v.]). Peaceful and prosperous, according to the *Encyclopaedia Britannica*.

Shortly after independence in 1967, Botswana issued this stamp, one of an attractive set of fourteen. The crested barbet (q.v. Angola) is one of eighty sub-species of barbet.

BOYACÁ

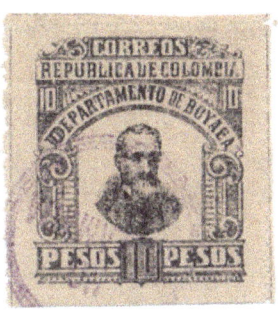

El Presidente **Marroquín**
Looks rather pale and rather thín.

A member of the Granadine Confederation, which went on to become one of Colombia's thirty-two *departamentos,* Boyacá is famous for the eponymous battle fought in 1819, in which South American insurgents were victorious over Spanish forces, paving the way for Colombian independence. José Manuel Marroquín (1827—1908), twice president of Colombia, features in this poorly executed stamp. He looks thin and haggard, as well he might: his period in office coincided with a lengthy civil war as well as Panama's secession from Colombia.

BRAZIL

**The thrill in Brazil
Is in cycling downhill.**

Brazil's emergence as a modern democracy did not follow the Bolivarian model of the Spanish-speaking countries of South America, with their pattern of independence in 1810 (or thereabouts), followed by years of caudillo-led chaos, conservatism and liberalism in equal measure.

Modern Brazilian stamp design is rather good, but the stamp shown here is typical of hundreds produced in the 1950s and 1960s, many of them undistinguished portraits of worthies, with poor perforations to boot.

BRITISH ANTARCTIC TERRITORY

**In times of slush,
Cry 'Mush!'**

In 1962 parts of the former Falkland Islands Dependencies, such as the South Orkney and South Shetland Islands – and a lot of sea – were amalgamated to form the British Antarctic Territory. The population of between fifty and one hundred presumably includes the resident full-time Postmaster General. This attractive 1963 stamp does not follow the early QEII issues in terms of design; philatelically speaking it thinks outside the box.

BRITISH COMMONWEALTH OCCUPATION FORCE

**Kangaroo with overprint:
War is over, take the hint.**

Forty thousand Australian, British, Indian and New Zealand military personnel occupied Japan from 1945 to 1952: this was the British Commonwealth Occupation Force (BCOF). For most of the period Australia contributed the majority of the BCOF's personnel, and an Australian always filled the position of commanding officer, which presumably explains why an Australian and not a British stamp was overprinted.

BRITISH EAST AFRICA

**This agèd queen and her pet lions
Are thinking of her numerous scions.**

British East Africa comprised territories that became today's Kenya, Uganda and Tanzania. 'British penetration of the area began at Zanzibar in the last quarter of the nineteenth century. In 1888 the Imperial British East Africa Company established claims to territory in what is now Kenya. In 1890 and 1894 British protectorates were established over the sultanate of Zanzibar and the kingdom of Buganda (Uganda) respectively, and in 1895 the company's territory in Kenya was transferred to the crown as the East Africa Protectorate … under the Treaty of Versailles Britain was awarded the former German territory of Tanganyika as a League of Nations mandate.' (*Encyclopaedia Britannica*)

BRITISH FORCES IN EGYPT

**King Fuad I, but who's he kidding?
He comes and goes at London's bidding.**

Egypt gained nominal independence from the British Empire as the Kingdom of Egypt in 1922, with Fuad I as king. Four matters were reserved to the British government's discretion, namely the security of imperial communications, defence, the protection of foreign interests and minorities, and Sudan. Never popular, Fuad felt insecure and was therefore prepared to intrigue with either the nationalists or the British in order to secure his position and powers. Fuad died soon after this stamp was issued and was succeeded by the young and dynamic Farouk.

BRITISH GUIANA

Indian shooting fish:
Time for a tasty dish.

British Guiana has pride of place in philately owing to the 1c Magenta, the world's most valuable stamp* (only one copy exists) and also one of the ugliest. It came into being owing to a temporary shortage of stamps: the postmaster had 1c and 4c values printed as stop-gaps, crude imitations of the usual stamps on sale. The story goes that one of the owners of the 1c Magenta possessed two copies but had one destroyed in order to increase the value of the lucky survivor.

The stamp featured above exudes a *Swallows and Amazons* paternalism – in the Amazon itself.

*When last sold in June 2021, it fetched a mere £6,000,000 and loose change, far less than expected.

BRITISH HONDURAS

**British Honduras as was,
Now it's Belize — because.**

In common with most Commonwealth countries, British Honduras issued attractive pictorial sets from 1938 onwards. This 1968 stamp, one of fourteen depicting flora and fauna, dispenses with the Queen's portrait, contenting itself with the royal initials surmounted with a crown. This practice is seen in other British colonial issues post-George VI.

BRITISH INDIAN OCEAN TERRITORY

**Lived a lionfish in deep waters,
Fathered many sons and daughters.**

The British government's removal from the Chagos Islands of the native Chagossians between 1967 and 1973 has turned out to be a thorn in its side ever since. Its refusal to grant the right of return to the largest island, Diego Garcia, on account of the US airbase stationed there, has recently earned it much opprobrium. Not only that: Mauritius claims that in exchange for its independence in 1968 it was forced to give up claims to the archipelago.

Whatever the thickness of the plot, this stamp, the highest value in a set of eighteen dedicated to marine life, is a stunner.

BRITISH LEVANT

**There's something venereal
About all this imperial.**

This stamp was overprinted for use at British post offices in the Turkish Empire. We have already seen that Austria, in common with a handful of other nations, distrusted the Ottoman postal service and instituted its own. Britain did the same. Here we have a nice tuppence ha'penny purple and blue issued for Queen Victoria's Silver Jubilee in 1887, showing an incongruously young Victoria, complete with appropriate overprint in Turkish currency.

BRITISH OCCUPATION OF ITALIAN COLONIES

**Mussolini, ducal plight,
Giving up without a fight.**

Definitive British stamps overprinted M.E.F. (Middle East Forces) were intended for British forces fighting the Italians in Eastern Libya in 1942. They were also available in Eritrea, Ethiopia (q.v.), Somalia (q.v.), and Tripolitania, as well as in the Dodecanese Islands. In 1950, the remaining overprinted stamps were made valid for postage throughout the UK.

BRITISH POST OFFICES IN CHINA

**If I were you
I'd learn Kung Fu.**

British Weihaiwei, on the north-eastern coast of China, was a leased territory of Great Britain from 1898 until 1930. In 1917 George V Hong Kong stamps such as the one featured here were overprinted for use in the territory. In 1909 the then Governor of Hong Kong, Sir Frederick Lugard, fresh from his governorship of Nigeria, proposed (unsuccessfully) that Britain end its lease in Weihaiwei in return for perpetual rule in Hong Kong.

Note the clipped edge on the lefthand side of the stamp, probably due to an over-zealous scissors-wielding individual tasked to remove thousands of stamps for a 'missionary mix'.

BRITISH VIRGIN ISLANDS

**Coronation of a king.
Tonic? With a little gin?**

Known as the sailing capital of the Caribbean, these former sugar islands are now a tax haven. The abolition of slavery, combined with the rise in the cultivation of sugar beet in Europe, spelt economic ruin for the Virgin Islands, as they are now known. This handsome stamp, issued in 1937 to mark the coronation of George VI, was standard issue for virtually all of the British Colonies. It exudes an air of benevolence and stability following the constitutional crisis brought about by Edward VIII, but in fact the British Empire was on its last legs.

BRUNEI

**They exult in the Sultan of Brunei,
A nice guy.**

A former British protectorate, this Islamic sultanate situated on the island of Borneo (whose name is derived from 'Brunei') has been independent since 1984. Once a powerful empire, Brunei lost territory to the Dutch and British and suffered the ignominy of seeing itself split in two, much like the Angolan and Russian enclaves of Cabinda and Kaliningrad respectively. The present sultan (not the one shown here) is wealthy to the tune of $28 billion; the country's considerable wealth is down to large reserves of oil and natural gas.

BULGARIA

**Eleven hundred years, this plane tree:
Bulgaria's pride, let us agree.**

Some years ago, I visited friends in Ruse, a small Bulgarian town on the Danube. I was struck by the beautiful if dilapidated Art Nouveau architecture, and the yoghurt, surely the best in the world. As a boy, this was one of my favourite stamps: I still find it striking. Otherwise (with the exception of the 1910 pictorial set), Bulgarian stamps are rather uninspiring.

BUNDI

**Agnus Dei,
Qui tollis peccata Bundi.**

Part of Rajasthan, and named after a thirteenth-century chieftain, Bundi is known for its stunning style of painting. The stamps of each feudatory state, of which Bundi was one, were valid only within that state, so that letters sent *outside* the state needed additional British India postage.

Some thought has gone into this design featuring strictly-not-dancing cattle, even if the execution leaves a little to be desired. The poorly applied SERVICE overprint indicates that it was intended for administrative use.

BURKINA FASO

**Upper Volta once it was,
Now it's called Burkina Fas.**

Formerly the French colony of Upper Volta *(Haute-Volte),* Burkina Faso means 'Land of Incorruptible People'. In common with some other sub-Saharan countries, Burkina Faso has experienced several coups and is now ruled by a military regime.

Based on an ornithological painting by John J. Audubon, this fine stamp, designed in Switzerland, promised great things to come.

Alas.

BURMA

**I spy with my little eye
The mighty bridge on the River Kwai.**

During WWII the Burmese welcomed the Japanese as liberators. This may seem hard to understand, but British disregard for Burma's ancient social, political and religious system was deeply resented. Worse still, in the eyes of the Indian Office, Burma simply did not exist as an entity. As a result, it was excluded from the constitutional arrangements proposed to India.

This handsome stamp, part of a set celebrating the country's first anniversary of independence in 1949, heralded a return to traditional values.

CAMEROON

***Kamerun* in German, *Cameroun* in French,
Rhymes like these will surely make a poetaster blench.**

Cameroon's name is derived from the Portuguese *Rio dos Camarões* ('River of Prawns'). It was colonised by the Germans, then by Britain and France concurrently, when they both seized the country from Germany in 1916. Britain's tenure was one of neglect; the French portion was thriving at the time of independence in 1960.

This stamp is one of a very attractive set featuring indigenous fauna; the design, as was common with newly independent French colonies in Western Africa, was French.

CANADA

**Halifax and Montreal,
Nice big country, space for all.**

Canada was once considered a drain on the British exchequer. I have very fond memories of singing Stravinsky in the Banff Centre in Alberta in 1996; I remember wangling large helpings in the canteen by speaking French to the Québécois staff.

The charm of many of the British colonial issues of the 1930s is absent in many of Canada's earlier stamps, for the most part very dreary. This easy-on-the-eye 1937 stamp featuring Halifax Harbour is a welcome change.

CANTON

A Treaty Port in Southern China;
Of all the ports I know, none fina.

Canton is the anglicisation of Guangzhou, capital of Guangdong, southern China, the first Chinese port to be regularly visited by European traders. It was the scene of the First Opium War, one of the most disgraceful episodes in British colonial history. Its most illustrious son was Sun Yat-Sen.

This attractive stamp (at least the part you can see under the postmark) features a Cambodian girl and was used at the French Indo-Chinese Post Office, which closed in 1922.

CAPE JUBY

**Ruby ports and finest sherries
Ferries carry to Cape Juby.**

Part of the Spanish Protectorate of Morocco, ceded to Spain in 1799 and returned (not without a fight) to Morocco in 1958. Most of the issues (Spanish stamps overprinted) were produced in larger quantities than the residents of Cape Juby could ever possibly have used, such as this one depicting a suitably regal Queen Victoria Eugénie. The stamp is incongruously inscribed 'Waterlow & Sons Ltd. Londres'.

CAPE OF GOOD HOPE

**The Cape of Good Hope
Is my favourite trope.**

In 1888 Cecil Rhodes, Governor of the Cape Colony, was pressing the British government for permission to push the Cape Colony far to the north, as part of his vision of colouring the entire map of Africa red.

This iconic stamp features an allegorical figure of 'Hope' leaning on an anchor, with Table Mountain in the background. It was unusual for British colonial stamps of the period (this one was issued in 1880) not to feature Queen Victoria. Perhaps 'Hope' was intended to represent her.

CAPE VERDE ISLANDS

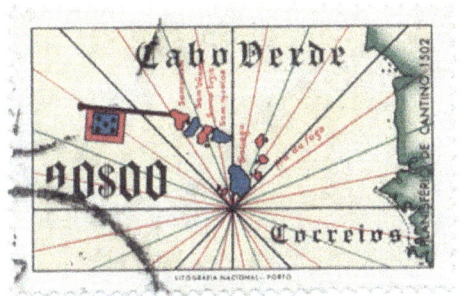

**A Portuguese possession,
An insular concession.**

A Portuguese colony until 1975, Cape Verde's prosperity, founded on the transatlantic slave trade, declined following abolition. The islands also served as a place of exile for political prisoners as well as a refuge for Jews and other victims of the Portuguese Inquisition. The islands' path to full national autonomy was bloody, as was usually the case with Portugal's colonies.

This 1952 stamp features an early sixteenth-century map of the islands, which makes it plain that there can be little doubt as to their ownership.

CAROLINE ISLANDS

Karolinen, **actually;**
Better to be factually.

The Caroline Islands make up today's republics of Palau and the Federated States of Micronesia. They were sold to Germany after the 1898 Spanish-American War, only to be seized by Japan in 1914.

Genuine used stamps are quite rare, owing to the relatively small number of letters written during the short German tenure. Germany issued these devil-may-care stamps featuring the Kaiser's yacht *Hohenzollern* for all its colonies. The design looks for all the world like the cover of a Tintin album.

CAYMAN ISLANDS

**Fiscal isles of ill repute,
Handy place to hide your loot.**

High up on the EU blacklist of tax havens,* the Cayman Islands have a high cost of living, making life difficult for those working in the service industries. The islands were named after the Spanish word for alligators, *caimanes,* spotted by Spanish explorers, the first they had ever seen.

This heavily postmarked 1900 stamp features elements of what I take to be local flora. The halfpenny rate suggests it may have been used on a postcard.

Five European countries also make it on to the list: the Netherlands, Switzerland, Ireland, Luxembourg and Cyprus.

CENTRAL AFRICAN EMPIRE

**Heart of Darkness, like a vampire
Stretched the power of this empire.**

Jean-Bédel Bokassa was president of the Central African Republic (1966–76) and self-styled Emperor of the Central African Empire (1976–79). Wikipedia tells us that – wait for it – 'In 1987, he was cleared of charges of cannibalism, but found guilty of the murder of schoolchildren and other crimes.'

Dictators are fond of basking in the reflected glory of their moral superiors, such as Rabindranath Tagore – as long as they're dead. This slickly produced miniature sheet (definitely not for the man on the street) is a good example.

CENTRAL AFRICAN REPUBLIC

**Formerly Ubangi-Shari,
Visited by Good Prince Harry.**

Despite possessing considerable mineral resources, the Central African Republic is among the ten poorest countries in the world. The Kongo-Wara rebellion of 1928 was kept quiet by the French government for fear it would undermine the 'achievements' of colonialism back home, which makes French intervention in the recent civil war there ironic, to say the least.

    I have a soft spot for stamp designs that are based on paintings, such as this one commemorating George Stephenson.

CENTRAL LITHUANIA

**Once 'twas free, now part of Poland;
It tried to annex Heligoland.**

The politically febrile period following WWI gave rise to many new states of short duration, such as the Republic of Central Lithuania, a Polish puppet republic created in 1920 without international recognition. It was founded following Żeligowski's Mutiny, when soldiers of the Polish army attacked the newly independent Lithuania during the Polish-Russian war.

This charming homespun postage due stamp features St Stanislaus's Cathedral in Vilnius. I have left the scissors job as it is; cutting out imperforate stamps must have been the bane of postal staff the world over.

CEYLON

**Ceylon's black tea, a pungent brew,
To King & Empire always true.**

A not-so-subtle shift takes place in British colonial stamp design from the reign of George V onwards: in addition to the monarch's portrait, we are told something about the place that is being ruled, even if the tone is paternalistic. This charmingly engraved scene, for example, features a tea-picker, doubtless working for a pittance. The decorated frame on the left-hand side of the stamp is probably a passing reference to Ceylonese sculpture.

Colonials considered Ceylon (now Sri Lanka) a plum posting on account of its felicitous climate.

CHAD

**It ain't that bad
Being born in Chad.**

Pádraig Carmody, author of the excellent *The New Scramble for Africa,* writes that at its height the war in the Democratic Republic of Congo involved seven African states: Rwanda, Uganda, Burundi, Namibia, Angola, Zimbabwe and Chad.

Poorly designed, cheaply engraved, with gaudy colours and a stubby overprint: not much going for this stamp, dating from the French colonial period and issued in 1924. Post-independence issues fare slightly better, although a 1969 issue featuring the frozen meat industry must have been a tough call for the designer.

CHAMBA

**The *viola da gamba*
Was invented in Chamba.**

During the Raj, postal union by a state was considered a sign of fealty to the British Empire. The privilege was reserved for the convention states, relatively few in number compared to the feudatory states, and gave the right to depict the sovereign on stamps. This design, a mixture of the restrained and the flamboyant, is based on the portrait of Queen Victoria aged fifteen as shown on the Penny Black (q.v.), from a sketch by Henry Corbould. Chamba, in the State of Himachal Pradesh in the Himalayas, is noted for its Pahari paintings.

CHARKHARI

**A state of India, long ago;
Its GDP was only so-so.**

Charkhari, on the other hand, was a feudatory state, part of Uttar Pradesh. It supported the British in the 1857 Mutiny and was awarded the privilege of an eleven-gun salute for its pains.
  Charkhari produced its own stamps, uniformly horrid.

CHILE

**Longest country in the world:
Thinnish, true, but quite uncurled.**

Chile has issued stamps since 1853, the first being inscribed 'Colon Chile', or 'Columbus Chile'; the idea that the Americas were inhabited at the time of Columbus's 'discovery' was – and remains – a hard sell as far as Western hegemony is concerned.

This stylised Dornier Wal monoplane and compass comes from a set of airmail stamps issued in 1934, a distinct improvement on earlier issues, falling as they do into the category of dull South American stamps. Modern Chilean issues tend to be fussy and over-coloured.

CHINA

**You've got a letter under sail?
Please check to see it's not junk mail.**

Issued shortly after the creation of the Chinese Republic in 1912, this delightful stamp features a junk (a Chinese sailing vessel of unknown origin, still in wide use). The bilingual inscription is probably due to an initial desire to be recognised by the outside world; a few years later, English disappears altogether from Chinese stamps.

CHRISTMAS ISLAND

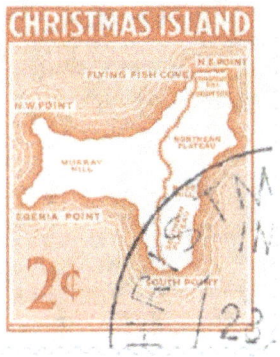

**This island has, despite its name,
A climate more like unto Spain.**

Christmas Island, lying roughly 200 miles south of Singapore, is administered as an external territory of Australia. The main settlement and attractively named port is at Flying Fish Cove, shown on this stamp, whose design reminds me of a basking shark. It was named on Christmas Day 1643 by the British East India Company. Probably best known for the annual invasion of millions of red crabs.

Christmas Island issued its first stamps in 1958; this stamp comes from a 1963 pictorial set which includes one entitled 'raising phosphate'. Phosphate was once the economic mainstay of the island.

CILICIA

**Great Snakes! This stamp is not familia:
Cilicia is not Sicilia.**

Known locally as Çukurova, Cilicia is a Turkish province bordering the Mediterranean Sea. Under the terms of the Armistice of Mudros that was signed in 1918 between the Ottoman Empire and the Allies, the Ottomans ceded the control of Cilicia to France. A power struggle then ensued between France and Turks loyal to Kemal Atatürk, with a large Armenian population stuck uncomfortably in the middle. Returning Armenians negotiated with France to establish the autonomous State of Cilicia, which lasted just three years. This standard 1920 French stamp nicknamed 'The Sower', overprinted O.M.F. *(Occupation Militaire Française),* tells us nothing whatever about 'Cilicie'.

CISKEI

**Ciskei's in
The Bay of Biscay.**

One of the Bantustan Republics, created in 1981 and dismantled in 1994 following the collapse of apartheid South Africa. The name Ciskei means 'on this side of the Kei River'. Xhosa people were forcibly resettled in the Ciskei and treated as a source of cheap labour. This stamp was issued in the same year as the republic's founding and comes from a set of twenty-three decently designed stamps on an ornithological theme.

COCHIN

**Maharaja Rama Varma
Looks as though he had good karma.**

Kochi, formerly Cochin, is a city on the Malabar Coast in Kerala State, southwestern India. Settled in turn by the Chinese, Portuguese, Dutch and British, it was one of the feudatory states of the Raj and issued its own rather attractive stamps, even if the Maharaja Rama Varma III looks as if butter wouldn't melt in his mouth. Wikipedia tells us that 'he showed keen interest in religious and spiritual matters.' A seventeenth-century account of Cochin under Portuguese rule by François Pyrard de Laval describes an idyllic colonial integration: 'The king and the inhabitants, as well Nairs as Moucois and other Malabars, Gentiles and Mahometans, agree well with the Portuguese and live in peace.'

COCHIN-CHINA

**This particular colonial outpost
Lies approximately on the south coast.**

A French colony in southern Indo-China, today's Vietnam.

As surcharges go, the ugliest in my collection. A surcharge usually indicates either that stocks have run low, or that inflation has forced a pricing rethink. This 25c 'Mouchon' French stamp (named after the designer, Louis-Eugène Mouchon) gets a hideous 5c workover, so badly executed that the '2' in the original '25' is still clearly visible.

COCOS (KEELING) ISLANDS

**I have a dream that, based on feeling,
I'll never go to Cocos (Keeling).**

With a population of just 544 and an area of five square miles, this tiny territory's justification for issuing stamps seems pretty slender; technically it is part of Australia. The first British explorers in the 1820s imported Malays to work the coconut plantations. In 1903 the islands were granted to the Clunies-Ross family in perpetuity, but the family's authority (they were nicknamed the 'Kings of the Cocos') was relinquished to Australia in 1978. This stamp, useful if you should lose your way while visiting, is part of the first set, issued in 1963.

I never did understand the 'Keeling' bit.

COLOMBIA

**Creative acts make one a-weary,
Although Bochica was a deary.**

Colombia's regional diversity meant that certain areas became virtually independent in the 1800s. Colombia's recent history has been dominated not so much by rivalry between oligarchies and the Left (a feature common to most South American countries) as between the state and the drug cartels.

The early issues are the usual dull coats of arms stuff, but there is a really lovely pictorial set dating from 1954. This charmingly stylised stamp was issued in 1938 for the Quincentenary of Bogotá. It features Bochica, the founding father of the Muisca people; according to legend, he brought them agriculture, laws and a moral code.

CONFEDERATE STATES OF AMERICA

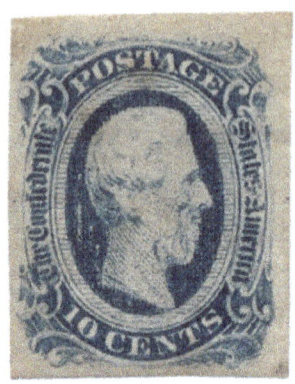

**Jefferson Davis and Reverend Amos
Committed war crimes now considered quite heinous.**

Owing to its short duration only nine stamps were issued for the Confederacy, including one printed by De la Rue in London (Britain, dependent on cotton, supported the Confederacy). Unsurprisingly the stamps are all portraits of Confederate worthies, or figures who might have been deemed posthumously sympathetic to the cause: Jefferson Davis himself, and Presidents Washington, Jackson and Jefferson. They are uniformly dreary.

CONGO (BRAZZAVILLE)

**Printing textiles, Brazzaville.
Worth a packet – half a mill?**

Formerly a French possession named Middle Congo, the Republic of Congo (Brazzaville) is so named to distinguish it from its huge neighbour, the Democratic Republic of Congo. The Republic of Congo's capital is named after the French-Italian explorer Brazza. Brazza himself had philanthropic tendencies, but the concessionary companies that followed him left no stone unturned when it came to extorting labour from the locals for the production of cash crops. The building of the Congo-Ocean Railway cost between 15,000 and 20,000 African lives.

This attractive 1970 stamp incorporates a textile motif in its frame.

CONGO (KINSHASA)

**This country, which is now Zaire,
Is faced with problems all too clear.**

Of all colonial records in Africa, Belgium's is surely the worst. A curious reluctance in Belgium to remove statues of Leopold II can only be attributed to an unwillingness to admit and apologise for the genocide that took place in the king's personal fiefdom (although placatory noises have been made recently). One of Africa's richest regions in terms of mineral wealth, it was rubber (and, prior to that, ivory) that fuelled the king's avarice; his regime of forced labour at the hands of concessionary companies led to murder and mutilation on a grand scale. In modern times the country has never really enjoyed any semblance of stability, for which the colonial legacy is largely to blame.

COOK ISLANDS

**Raratonga, lovely name,
Deserves, I think, a bit more fame.**

Recent Cook Islands' issues are chock-a-block with the Royal Family, but this 1920 stamp is quite delightful, even if the underlying message – the landing of Captain Cook – presages colonialism. The vignette shows Cook's ship quite out of scale with the rest of the design; the local inhabitants appear enthusiastic. The frame is redolent of native sculpture, such as one might find in a Raratongan canoe: scrolls and chisel marks galore.

COSTA RICA

**President Soto
Presided *in toto*.**

Bernardo Soto Alfaro (1854—1931) was president of Costa Rica from 1885 to 1890. He was responsible for establishing free, compulsory secular education, as well as separating church and state. Unfortunately, he meddled in the election of 1890 and was forced to cede victory to his opponent. Here he is given the full engraved job, complete with curls and swirls that remain within the realm of the reasonable.

CRETE

**Not Thetan,
But *Cretan*.**

Formerly a Turkish possession, from 1898 until 1908 Crete found itself under the joint protection (read: vested interests) of Britain, France, Italy and Russia (joint meetings must have been a lot of fun). Turkey recognised Greece's claim to the island in 1913.

Many of Crete's stamps, such as this fine depiction of Triton, were based on mythology. Triton was the son of Poseidon and Amphitrite, god and goddess of the sea respectively.

CROATIA

**Of *Split* and *Zagreb* will I tell,
Dubrovnik's glut of tourists: hell.**

This stamp was issued in 1941, when Croatia was allied with the Axis. The relatively poor lithography is no advertisement for the beauty of Dubrovnik, although nowadays, post-*Game of Thrones,* no publicity is needed. Later post-independence issues are well designed and worth exploring.

CUBA

Tuba mirum, spargens sonum:
Cuban rum is *mucho bonum*.

At the time of this stamp's issue in 1899 Spain had just ceded Cuba to the US, following a war that has been vividly documented by Stephen Crane. The playful invocation of Cuba's putative merits, featuring lush plant life as well as a mythical sea creature framing the vignette of the liner *Umbria*, contributes to a very successful design. I discovered with surprise that steam ships regularly carried masts and auxiliary sails into the 1900s.

CUNDINAMARCA

**Cundinamarca, Cundinamarca,
Birthplace of the *Magna Carta!***

The path to South American independence was given a major boost by the news of Napoleon's successes in Spain in 1807. Cundinamarca was one of the states of the Granadine Federation that went on to become modern-day Colombia: new national boundaries were initially based around the borders of certain provinces such as Cundinamarca. None of which is particularly relevant to the appalling design of this 1885 stamp – is that an eagle? In fairness, it may well be a forgery. I recall school exam papers in the early 1970s printed on a Gestetner machine – they looked rather like this.

CURAÇAO

**Curaçao, in the Antilles…
The very name gives me the willies.**

A country within the Kingdom of the Netherlands, known for its eponymous liqueur made from orange peel, Curaçao has preserved much of its beautiful Dutch colonial architecture. Its prosperity was based on sugar, harvested, as ever, by slaves.

This Art Deco airmail stamp issued in 1931 is a masterpiece of design. One of a set of thirteen, it features a purposeful, stylised Mercury flanked by geese (or doves?). Airmail was a new and exciting phenomenon, which inspired some of philately's best designers.

CYPRUS

**1 piastre black & brown:
George V is back in town.**

The British policy of divide and rule in Cyprus, fostering ties with the Turks at the expense of the majority Greek population, left a legacy of bitter division. Britain left Cyprus ignominiously after a violent struggle.

The stamp featured above is one of the many British Commonwealth 'pictorials' issued during the reigns of George V, George VI and Elizabeth II from roughly the mid-1930s until the early 1960s. They are satisfyingly engraved, but on closer examination (i.e., when magnified) are not all of the same standard. All the same, they must have made a welcome change from those endless royal portraits.

CZECHOSLOVAK ARMY IN SIBERIA

**Whither now, O sentinel?
Vladivostok's a hard sell.**

Towards the end of WWI, the Czech Legion, numbering between 70,000 and 100,000, was encouraged to shift its efforts from the Eastern Front to France following the Bolshevik Revolution. However, the Legion's route westwards was barred, and it was decided that it should make its way to Vladivostok and await shipment to the Western Front. Its success in controlling the Trans-Siberian Railway in the face of Bolshevik offensives ensured its survival and eventual repatriation in 1920.

CZECHOSLOVAKIA

**I never wrote a bouncing Czech:
Online banking's more hi-tech.**

Most communist bloc stamp design was either dull or simply strident, but Czech design is the exception that proves the rule. Not even stamps featuring steroid-fed Olympic achievements or the endless perorations of Soviet space travel could dampen the artistic elan of this haven of philatelic excellence in the dark days of communist rule, and the tradition of excellent graphic design thrives post-1989. This charming 1919 vignette of Hradčany Castle (one of the first Czechoslovak stamps to be issued), is sheer delight. There is a childlike quality to the frame's arboreal elements, which one also finds in J.R.R. Tolkien's best illustrations.

DAHOMEY

**1c black and red on blue:
Dahomey, friend, was made for you.**

In the eighteenth and nineteenth centuries the Kingdom of Dahomey prospered from the slave trade in what is now southern Benin. In 1975 the name Dahomey was changed to Benin. This 'Tablet' key-type stamp (the first stamp issued for Dahomey, in 1899) proclaimed French hegemony through the allegorical figures of Peace and Commerce. A later issue from 1913 features no fewer than forty-five stamps of identical design: 'native climbing palm'. The 'black and red on blue' refers to the blueish paper on which the stamp is printed, although that colour is evident only on the back of the stamp.

DANISH WEST INDIES

**Virgin Islands USA:
Uncle Sam is here to stay.**

Also known as the Danish Virgin Islands, this small Danish Caribbean colony of four islands profited from the slave trade until abolition, at which point its economic doom was sealed. Denmark sold the islands to the US in 1917 for $25,000,000: they are now known as the US Virgin Islands.

This stamp owes its allure to the use of concentric circles incorporating four crowns and text, with the central portrait of the monarch a blue silhouette. The designer has seen fit to leave just enough surface unfilled, with the result that the stamp, for all its detail, has an airy, uncluttered feel about it. The currency is the bit, as in 'I ain't got two bits.'

DANZIG

**Teutonic knights and Hanseatic;
Gdansk it is now, more pragmatic.**

The Congress of Vienna in 1814 not only paved the way for a future Belgium, but also divided Poland between Russia, Austria and Prussia: as a result, Danzig (Gdansk) was relegated to the province of West Prussia. Under the Treaty of Versailles (1919) Danzig was awarded the status of a free city, until, in 1939, it refused Hitler's demand that it be handed over to Germany, which, more than anything else, kindled the spark that ignited WWII.

This delightful 1935 airmail issue, with its childlike bunting proclaiming FREIE STADT DANZIG, breathes insouciance.

DEDEAGATZ

**Dedeagatz, cor! What a name!
Now *that* baptism was a shame.**

The Sanjak of Dedeagatz or Dedeağaç was a second-level province (sanjak) of the Ottoman Empire in Thrace (q.v.), created in 1878. Occupied by Bulgarian troops in the First Balkan War (1912–13), it was later handed over to Greece, where it is known as Alexandroupoli.

This stamp, standard dull issue, was used in the French Post Office in Dedeağaç until 1914. The feeble overprint reads Dédéagh – presumably the Turkish spelling and pronunciation defeated the local ex-pats.

DENMARK

**Ancient kingdom, mostly flat,
Tivoli and Kattegat.**

The Scandinavian countries have never shied away from monochrome stamp design, and have produced some superb line-engraved stamps, tasteful and understated. This one, although multi-coloured, is a little gem. It features Denmark's Rebild Hills.

It's good to know that the original Lego bricks can still be used in modern Lego sets. And that Greenland is not for sale.

DHAR

**O my dharling, o my dharling,
O my dharling Clementine!**

Dhar, in the central state of Madhya Pradesh, owes its name to a toppled iron pillar dating from the thirteenth century (of all the owes-its-name-to stories, surely the oddest). Dhar houses the Raja Bhoja's school, built in the fourteenth or fifteenth century, whose paved slabs are covered with inscriptions teaching the rules of Sanskrit grammar.

This 1897 stamp is one of the 'Uglies' (let's call them cinema stubs) produced by feudatory states during the Raj; it gives no inkling of the splendid temples found in the region.

DIEGO-SUAREZ

**A port in Northern Madagascar.
Gee up, Jasper! Faster, Caspar!**

The French colonial outpost of Diego-Suarez (named after the Portuguese explorer Diogo Soares) was used as a coaling station by the French, who were granted a protectorate over the bay and surrounding area following the first Franco-Malagasy war (1883–85). It was the primary objective of Operation Ironclad, the starting point of the Allied invasion and capture of Madagascar during WWII.

The poor quality of the engraving in this 1894 stamp – particularly the crude insertion of the name of the protectorate – goes hand in hand with the poor centring, so that the upper perforations impinge on the stamp proper.

DJIBOUTI

**Come on Djibouti,
Shake yo' booty!**

A port in French Somaliland, later incorporated into the French Territory of the Afars and Issas, Djibouti was established as a coaling station for ships on their way to Indo-China. It was granted independence as Djibouti Republic in 1977. The engraving in this 1894 issue is not the finest, but in depicting Djibouti itself shows some interest in local culture, complete with idealised natives. Note how the word *centimes* has been abbreviated as *ces,* which is not usual, as well as the fake perforations: this is an imperforate stamp.

DJIBOUTI REPUBLIC

**Fancy boundless,
Soaring, groundless.**

Two-thirds of the population of this small country live in the eponymous capital. As the French colonial name implied, the Afars and Issas are two separate ethnic groups who do not always see eye to eye; this has led to a brief civil war (1992–94).

This striking 1982 airmail stamp commemorates the 1,350th anniversary of Mohammed's death, and features the mosque at Medina, a truly staggering edifice.

DOMINICA

**I wish I could finisha
Rhyme with Dominica.**

Violent altercations between the British and French have meant that Dominica has changed hands several times, achieving full independence in 1978. It owes its name to *Dies Dominica,* the Lord's Day, since Columbus first sighted it on a Sunday. Unusually for a British ex-colony, it has remained Roman Catholic, doubtless owing to the French presence on the island.

Dominica's outstanding natural beauty, especially its spectacular mountainous topography, has impressed generations of nature lovers. The Layou River features in this attractive stamp, issued in 1954.

DOMINICAN REPUBLIC

**Hispaniola 'tis, but less the Haiti,
Peopled by the haigh and maighty.**

The Dominican republic forms the larger portion of the island of Hispaniola, bordering Haiti. The earliest experiments in Spanish imperial rule were conducted here, leading to a cruel, exploitative slave-based society. Where to begin when it comes to cataloguing the further terrible oppression suffered by this small country? The dictatorship of Rafael Trujillo (1930–61) in particular stands out for its cruelty. Through all this, decent stamp design has managed to survive, and some issues are really quite attractive, in itself unusual for Central America. The San Rafael Bridge, the largest suspension bridge in the Antilles (EL MAYOR DE LAS ANTILLAS), is commemorated here.

DUBAI

**Don't be shy…
It's me – Dubai!**

In marked contrast to the Dominican Republic, Dubai seems to have escaped civil strife and war. Oil revenues have helped finance tax-free salaries and some remarkable building projects, including the Palm Jumeirah, a man-made island in the shape of a palm tree. Until its incorporation into the United Arab Emirates (q.v.) in 1971, Dubai issued its own stamps, but can hardly be said to have covered itself in philatelic glory. This 1968 stamp features the Atlas Moth, one of the largest in the world.

ECUADOR

**Did Quito
Invent the *mojito*?**

Known for its environmental diversity and Panama hats (so named because they were worn by Ecuadorian workers constructing the Panama Canal), Ecuador's early history was tormented. From 1822 to 1830 it was a member of the confederation of Gran Colombia, together with what are now the countries of Panama, Colombia and Venezuela.

Some stamp designer somewhere was contracted to produce almost all of South and Central America's early stamps. These are uniformly dull, featuring overloaded coats of arms, bloated eagles and presidential worthies. This attractive stamp is different: it comes from a 1935 set commemorating the centenary of Darwin's visit to the Galapagos Islands.

EGYPT

**Pharaonic, Luxory cruises,
Pyramids and feline muses.**

Having dislodged the Ottoman Empire while at the same time quashing French territorial ambitions in the country, Britain established a protectorate in Egypt from 1882 to 1952. The British were always reluctant to possess Egypt in the full sense of the word: a protectorate usually meant the protecting of the interests of the *protector* without investing large sums of money in the protected. Britain saw itself as the benefactor of a down-trodden peasantry, while at the same time denying high office to Egyptians. But no colonial argy-bargy is evident in this fine 1914 stamp, one of a set commemorating the splendours of Ancient Egypt: the Colossi of Amenophis III at Thebes.

EL SALVADOR

El Salvador, *The Saviour!*
***(I* ain't misbehaviour.)**

'Only El Salvador produces the Peru Balsam' is the somewhat puzzling inscription on this attractive 1924 stamp (in fact the species is native to the country). El Salvador is the smallest and most densely populated of the Central American nations. A coup in 1931 saw the installation of a succession of military governments that controlled the country through 1979; subsequent US meddling in El Salvador's affairs merely served to aggravate the country's misery. On a more positive note, it appears a very picturesque place, with the Cerro Verde volcano a must-see.

ESTONIA

**Estonia, now, has a lovely capital,
Tallinn its name, a town most affable.**

Modern Estonian stamps are sophisticated and colourful, but there is a charm about Estonia's early issues, dating from its first period as an independent country from 1918 to 1940 (having successfully fought off Bolshevik attempts to impose Soviet rule).

This view of Tallinn exudes a kind of homemade charm, although the scroll and meshwork are subtle enough. Somebody was in a hurry to cut this stamp from the sheet: a real hatchet-job.

ETHIOPIA

**Never colonised, now that's a record:
Down on your knees, the Lord's your Shepherd.**

Ethiopia and Liberia are the only two African countries never to have been colonised (apart from a few years under Italian rule in the case of Ethiopia). Ethiopia's victory over Italian forces at the Battle of Adwa in 1896 was the greatest humiliation suffered by any colonial power in Africa.

Under Emperor Haile Selassie, Ethiopia saw great improvements to infrastructure and public services.

The Ethiopian alphabet is part of the attraction of this 1966 airmail stamp featuring the endangered Walia ibex.

FALKLAND ISLANDS

**Black-necked swan on penny red,
Chilly waters (no Club Med).**

The first recorded landing on the Falkland Islands was made in 1690 by John Strong, who named them after a British naval officer, Viscount Falkland. They were first settled by the French, who called them the *Malouines*. The British were the first to settle West Falkland, but were expelled by the Spanish, who in turn abandoned the islands under the threat of war. British administration was consolidated in 1833. A fact not generally known is that Britain in the 1970s was keen on the idea of the islands entering into some kind of association with Argentina, since they were proving a drain on the British exchequer.

The 1933 centenary issue is one of the most beautiful of all British colonial sets. This stamp, issued in 1938, is very adroitly engraved.

FALKLAND ISLANDS DEPENDENCIES

**South Georgia and South Sandwich Islands:
Rugged coasts and craggy highlands.**

Now known as the British Antarctic Territory (q.v.), this huge area included poetic-sounding islands such as the South Orkneys and South Shetlands.

This handsome schooner was named, intriguingly, the *Wyatt Earp*. Built in 1919 in Norway, she was originally called the *Fanefjord*. Sold to a certain Lincoln Ellsworth in 1933, she was renamed after the famous sheriff of Tombstone. The *Wyatt Earp* surveyed the inhospitable but spectacular Balleny Islands at the eastern extremity of the Australian Antarctic Territory. She was lost off the coast of Queensland in 1959.

FAROE ISLANDS

**Rather far-flung, Isles of Faroe,
Quite a chilly archipelago.**

A spectacular archipelago, almost treeless, a cross between Iceland and Scotland. The temperature never rises above 17°C in summer. My sort of place, in a nutshell.

Faroese stamps are for the most part interesting and exuberantly coloured. This 1986 stamp is one of a set with a bridge theme: here Leypnangjogv Bridge is given a sober pencil-sketch treatment. Notice how the postmark adds to the effect.

FEDERATED MALAY STATES

**British Protectorate in South East Asia,
Now it's called (I think) Malaysia.**

Philately hammers home the message that many countries were once made up of a tapestry of smaller statelets before unification: among others, Germany, Colombia, Italy, Australia, and … Malaysia. The Federated Malay States, established in 1896, initially comprised Selangor, Perak, Pahang and Negri Sembilan, before expanding to include thirteen states, but full Malaysian unification did not take place until 1963. Singapore seceded (at Malaysia's request) in 1965, and Brunei preferred to go it alone. The states of Johore, Kedah, Kelantan, Perlis and Terengganu chose not to join the federation in 1896, and remained under British protection.

FERNANDO PÓO

**How do you dó,
Fernando Póo?**

The island of Bioko, also called Fernando Po, or Fernando Póo, lies northwest of continental Equatorial Guinea, of which it is part. Curiously, the capital, Malabo, is situated on the island, and not on mainland Equatorial Guinea. For a short time, it was used by the British as an antislavery base. Fernando Póo and Rio Muni (q.v.), both Spanish colonies, merged to form Equatorial Guinea in 1968.

This 1907 stamp features the young King Alfonso XIII of Spain, who acceded to the throne in 1902 at the age of sixteen. His constant interference in Spanish parliamentary matters gave rise to extreme political instability, with no fewer than thirty-three governments being formed between 1902 and 1933, all of which was grist to Franco's mill.

FIJI

**Native village far away,
Placid king in nice array.**

Fiji's first issues, dating from 1870, were issued by the local newspaper, the *Fiji Times,* and bore the monogram of the local king. The British consul objected, and two years later the first colonial stamps were issued. Pictorial stamps appeared in 1891, which is very early on the philatelic time scale. The George VI issues for the British Commonwealth, mostly dating from 1938, the year following his accession, seldom disappoint. Note the indigenous-looking 'teeth' (a decorative pattern on a canoe, possibly) which surround this lovely vignette.

FINLAND

**Poised and suave and slightly slinky
Sits the harbour of Helsinki.**

Finland's first issues are Russian, since it was a Russian Grand Duchy until 1917. Multi-coloured issues make a reluctant appearance from the mid-1960s onwards, although I prefer the earlier finely engraved monochrome stamps, such as this one, a sober but airy 1942 view of Helsinki harbour basking in the spring sunshine. Finland always uses the Finnish and English versions of the country name on its stamps.

FIUME

**Postage due, you've more to pay:
Fret and fiume the livelong day.**

Fiume (present-day Rijeka, in Croatia) once belonged to Hungary, but was occupied by Allied Forces from 1918 to 1919, before becoming a 'free state' under the control of the fascist leader Gabriele D'Annunzio (q.v. Arbe). It was annexed to Italy in 1924 following the poet's downfall.

This is our first postage due stamp; they have now all but disappeared (these days insufficient postage usually means a trot down to the local post office to recover the item), but they continue to fascinate collectors. One of the more interesting sets.

FRANCE

**Feeble empire, pompous man,
Ended, sadly, in Sedan.**

What could be duller, really, than a stamp featuring a ruling head of state? This one, dating from 1853, features Napoleon III at the beginning of his reign; it is one of the better ones. It was used not only in metropolitan France but also in the colonies; separate colonial issues only appeared from 1877.

I find it hard to muster enthusiasm for most French and French colonial stamps: many of them seem fussy and over-designed, with rather bizarre colour schemes. Having said that, some of the better ones (including two superb designs by Henry Cheffer for Algeria and French West Africa) are out of bounds for reasons of copyright.

FRENCH POST OFFICES IN CHINA

This French stamp is overprinted:
Native seen through glass much tinted.

There were dozens of French post offices throughout Asia during the nineteenth century, the last one closing in 1940. Wikipedia puts it succinctly: 'The French post offices abroad were a global network of post offices in foreign countries established by France to provide mail service where the local services were deemed unsafe or unreliable. They were generally set up in cities with some sort of French commercial interest.' Unsafe or unreliable: I am sure we have all felt that from time to time about our own national postal services. As to the stamp, the inscription on the parchment (DROITS DE L'HOMME) gives much food for thought. The Chinese characters provide a welcome oriental touch.

FRENCH POST OFFICES IN MOROCCO

**25 cents on 25 cents?
Really, now, that makes no sense.**

An identical stamp to the preceding one, this time with an overprint in centimos, since Spanish currency was used in Morocco at the time of this stamp's issue in 1902 (the French shared territory with the Spanish protectorate). France was not yet 'protecting' Morocco – that began in 1912 and continued until 1956.

FRENCH POST OFFICES IN THE TURKISH EMPIRE

I got a dose of Ottomania
Writing home to Aunt Yesenia.

By the nineteenth century half a dozen European countries, including France, had been granted the right to maintain post offices within the Ottoman Empire. Initially restricted to consular mail, these post offices were later used by foreign and local businesses and individuals, provided they used the postage stamps of the post office concerned. The system came to an end with the Treaty of Lausanne in 1923.

The theatrical decor featured here would not have been out of place at the Opéra Garnier.

FRENCH SOMALI COAST

**If I were you, I wouldn't boast
About the French Somali Coast.**

The French Somali Coast was a precursor of Djibouti. Despite the rather distracting postmarks and faded colours, this stamp, featuring the mosque at Tadjoura, is a real charmer. It was designed by Paul Merwart, who died in the year of its issue (1902) in a volcanic eruption on Martinique.

GABON

**I think the loveliest place to be
Is under a Gabonese Tulip Tree.**

Gabon was part of French West Africa from 1937 until its independence in 1960. Thanks to its huge oil reserves Gabon is one of Africa's richest countries, although little of that wealth trickles down to the man on the street: many live on $2 a day.

Gabon's early issues incorporate some of the better features of French stamp design. The Gabonese Tulip tree shown here is native to the tropical dry forests of Africa. It has been nominated among the hundred worst plant invaders, but is very beautiful, nonetheless.

(THE) GAMBIA

**The Gambia, you know, is far from Zambia,
And farther still from Vietnambia.**

Mainland Africa's smallest country, Gambia owes its odd shape (long and narrow, entirely surrounded by Senegal) to colonial shenanigans between the British and French at the end of the nineteenth century (Britain twice tried to trade Gambia to France without success). As to the 'The' sometimes seen in the name, one rather mundane explanation is that (The) Gambia didn't want to be confused with (The) Zambia.

The cattle egret pictured on this stamp is a member of the heron family, and a very useful one too: it perches on cattle and rids its host of ticks and other noisome beasties.

GEORGIA

**A handsome frame, a clumsy drawing:
Georgia 'tis, towards statehood clawing.**

Many small countries (including Georgia) emerged in the Caucasus after WWI, all quickly swallowed by the bottomless maw of Bolshevik expansion. One might have thought Georgia's most notorious son, Joseph Stalin, would have treated it with relative leniency, but in fact the Kremlin ruled it with a fist of iron. Stalin's annexation of Georgia in 1921 was carried out without Lenin's approval.

This 1922 stamp, featuring a soldier, is a bit confused, although the frame is agreeable. Post-independence issues are vibrant if overcrowded.

GERMAN EAST AFRICA

**Germany, brief tenant here,
Left a country sad and sere.**

Germany arrived relatively late on the colonial scene, but during its brief thirty-year tenure (1884–1914) inflicted untold misery on the natives of its African colonies. In Togo, for instance, since oxen could not survive the climate, the locals were commandeered to pull huge wagonloads of cotton by hand; in East Africa, Robert Koch experimented on Africans with arsenic in his quest to find a cure for sleeping sickness. To top it all, strict racial segregation was the order of the day.

The Kaiser's yacht *Hohenzollern* sails blithely on.

GERMAN OCCUPATION OF BELGIUM

**Passchendaele, Mons and Wipers,
Kaiser Wilhelm's doughty fighters.**

Germany's failure to occupy the Belgian coast at the outset of WWI denied them maritime access to France, and played a small part in the Allied Forces' victory. The German army's savage bombardment of Louvain and the destruction of its library, following hot on the heels of the massacre in Dinant, remain in Belgian folk memory.

The portrait on this iconic stamp, issued in 1900 and designed by Paul Waldraff, features the allegorical figure of *Germania,* based on a portrait of the actress Anna Führing.

GERMAN OCCUPATION OF LORRAINE

**Europe's most disputed region,
Questionable adhesion.**

Today, Lorraine incorporates four French *départements* and a small Belgian region called the Gaume. Originally much bigger, being one of the three regions that formed Charlemagne's legacy established by the Treaty of Verdun in 843, it was named after either Emperor Lothair I or King Lothair. An idea of its original extent can be seen by perusing a map of the Western Front in WWI, which stretched from Nieuwpoort in Belgium to the Swiss border, all of which was once Lotharingia. Place names such as Metz and Strasbourg betray a Germanic provenance, so that this WWII stamp – to Germans at least – would have symbolised a reclaiming of what was Germany's by right.

GERMAN OCCUPATION OF POLAND, SORT OF

**Poland, where the World War started:
Panzers rolled when Hitler farted.**

At the outset of WWI, Polish territory was split between the Austro-Hungarian, German and Russian Empires, and became the scene of many operations on the Eastern Front. I have played fast and loose with history: this stamp was issued when Hitler was still at school. A shame about the ugly struck-through overprint, which almost obscures what is *au fond* a fine design. I had assumed that this was an occupation issue; in fact, the crossed-out Gen. Gouv. Warschau and the new Poczta Polska overprint tell us that this is 1918, and the Poles under General Piłsudski are very much in charge of their own destiny.

GERMAN POST OFFICES IN CHINA

**In Goethe's tongue the name of China
Rhymes with the much-loved semolina.**

More *Germania*, aka Anna Führing. And what an elegant overprint and surcharge, compared to the chunky effort on the Aitutaki stamp (q.v.), or the frightful botched job on that of Annam & Tonkin (q.v.). An imperial German Postal Agency was opened in the Shanghai Consulate in 1886, followed by dozens of others. They were all closed in 1917.

GERMAN POST OFFICES IN MOROCCO

**French and Spanish, German too –
Foreign land grabs through and through.**

… and the last of the *Germanias,* with an elegant colour scheme and a distinguished 'Sütterlin' overprint. German post offices were established in a host of Moroccan towns from 1899, using Spanish currency. The last one closed in 1919. Note that the original value, 30 Pfennig, is not obscured, as is the case with the previous stamp.

In fairness, I don't think that Germany grabbed any Moroccan land.

GERMAN POST OFFICES IN THE TURKISH EMPIRE

**What a disaster,
Being a piastre.**

German postal agencies opened in Constantinople in 1870. All were closed at the outset of WWI, which I find puzzling, since the Ottoman Empire was Germany's ally. This is a 'German Eagle' issued in 1899, complete with functional overprint in paras. (A piastre is not a para, but it's good for rhyming. The word means 'thin metal plate'.)

GERMAN SOUTH WEST AFRICA

**Took a boat trip to Namibia,
Tripped and fell and hurt my tibia.**

The German Protectorate of South West Africa was not originally a land grab, but came about following the sale of a tract of territory by locals to a Bremen merchant. The suppression of the Herero and Nama revolt in 1904/05 led to the extermination of twenty thousand people, who died of hunger in the desert. This was General Trotha's *Vernichtungsbefehl* and deserves to be notorious, but the fact is that the horrors of WWII have meant that Germany's colonial role prior to WWI is rarely discussed. Following Germany's capitulation to South African troops in 1915, South West Africa was administered by apartheid South Africa, attaining independence as Namibia only in 1990.

GERMANY (REICH)

**Bismarck's plan was plain to see:
Germany just *had* to be.**

Issues for the period from German unification until the end of WWII are usually referred to as *Reich*. This stamp is part of the very first set issued for the new country in 1872, and features an elegant if difficult-to-make-out embossed German imperial eagle, believed to have been used by Charlemagne. Engraved by H.G. Schilling, complete with a Frankfurt postmark.

Is that a rust stain I see?

GERMANY (WEIMAR REPUBLIC)

**Galloping inflation,
Not good for a nation.**

It must have been demoralising to have had to constantly surcharge stamps in Germany during its period of hyper-inflation in the 1920s (images of wheelbarrows full of almost worthless banknotes come to mind). But it was also a very rich period culturally: the biting satire of German cabaret spearheaded by Brecht and Weill, the svelte tones of the 'Comedian Harmonists', to say nothing of the German Expressionists' works, shortly to be termed by the Nazis *entartete Kunst,* or 'Degenerate Art'.

GERMANY (THIRD REICH)

**German opera's *heil'ger Gral*,
Known to all as Parsifal.**

Given Hitler's idolisation of Wagner, it is hardly a coincidence that this stamp, one of a series illustrating scenes from the operas, was issued in 1933. The designs, unlike most Third Reich stamps which are at least polished, are somewhat crude, giving no idea of the splendour of the music – and this one is the best of the set. Note the 35 Rpf *(Reichspfennig)* visible in the left-hand frame: this is a charity or *Nothilfe* stamp, available at a premium. (That'll be 75 Rpf, please.)

GERMANY
(ALLIED OCCUPATION)

Simple numbers, but the rubble
Was a source of toil and trouble.

Postal mayhem reigned in Germany at the end of WWII: along with everything else, post offices had been destroyed, including stocks of stamps and the infrastructure necessary for delivering letters. Stamps bearing the defaced effigy of Hitler were used where no others were available. Into the breach rode Allied Military Command, with simple designs based on numerals, wisely steering clear of themes that might have been construed as provocative. There were separate issues for the various zones of military occupation until 1949, when the Federal Republic was established.

GERMANY (DDR)

**Walther Ulbricht, Checkpoint Charlie;
Stasi thugs – why bother parley?**

The combination of the words democratic and republic in a country's name usually means that precisely those two qualities are markedly absent. Walther Ulbricht, inflexible and unlikeable, was the father of the Berlin Wall, the building of which, surprisingly, curried no favour with his Soviet masters and led to his fall from power.

East German stamps, apart from the numerous horrid propaganda issues, were among the better-designed of the communist bloc.

GHANA

***Fire-crowned Bishop,* lovely bird,
Ornithology's last word.**

Although relatively small in area and population, Ghana, the first sub-Saharan African country to achieve independence from colonial rule, is one of Africa's leading countries economically. Known as The Gold Coast (q.v.) before independence, owing to its gold reserves, it was once a hub for slave trading.

Ghana's early issues, of which this 1959 stamp is a good example, are exuberantly coloured and generally pleasing.

GIBRALTAR

**Straits of Gibraltar,
Where ships never falter.**

Spain formally ceded Gibraltar to Britain under the terms of the Treaty of Utrecht (1713), which brought to a close the War of the Spanish Succession. Attempts by Spain to retake it in the late eighteenth-century failed. Franco closed the border between 1969 and 1985, following a referendum that was overwhelmingly in favour of the 'Rock' remaining British. Its status remains a point of contention, particularly in the light of Brexit.

Some of the fizz has gone out of British colonial stamp design.

GILBERT & ELLICE ISLANDS

**Seascape, this, in blue and grey;
Ideal living, I would say.**

A former British protectorate and colony in the South Pacific which split on independence, the Gilbert Islands becoming Kiribati, the Ellice Islands Tuvalu. The Gilbert & Ellice Islands were a chain of sixteen atolls and coral islands in the western Pacific Ocean, now part of Micronesia. The Battle of Tarawa took place there in 1943.

As with most of the British colonial issues from 1938 to 1939, an attempt is made to incorporate features of local culture (or what passes for it) into the stamp's design – usually the frame – as in this attractive coastal scene.

GILBERT ISLANDS

**Islands loved by literati,
Changed their name to Kiribati.**

Following a referendum in 1974, the Gilbert & Ellice Islands decided to part company peacefully. Shortly afterwards the Gilbert Islands were renamed Kiribati (Kiribati, pronounced 'Kiribass', being a patois rendition of 'Gilberts'), while the Ellice Islands were renamed Tuvalu, meaning 'Eight standing together'.

GOLD COAST

***Northern Territories, Mounted Constabulary:*
What a geopolitical confabulary!**

Also known, less poetically, as the Slave Coast. Initially the British concentrated their colonial efforts in the coastal area of the Gold Coast, but after the Anglo-Ashanti wars* they occupied what is now the rest of Ghana as well.

The Gothic arch strikes one as incongruous, but may have been a reference to Islamic architecture, which of course invented it. About seventeen per cent of the population is Muslim.

*A series of five conflicts which took place between 1824 and 1900.

GREAT BRITAIN

**World's first stamp (no country name):
Dressed in black, this comely dame.**

The invention of the postage stamp in 1840 was as revolutionary in its way as that of the email. The design for the Penny Black was based on a sketch of Queen Victoria at the age of fifteen by Henry Corbould (1787—1844). The choice of black is perplexing, and nothing if not funereal. Perhaps it was felt it would be more difficult to forge the stamp; in any event, black was quickly replaced by red, since it was found that postmarks were not easy to see (as in my example), meaning that a stamp might be reused.

My Penny Black has rather tightly cut margins, thus reducing its value. Still, it is a cherished child.

GREECE

**Ancient stamp, urn older still:
Pallas Athene, Hellenic thrill!**

In terms of design, this stamp is light years away from the usual offerings that celebrate major sporting events: it marks the most prestigious of them all, the Olympic Games, on the occasion of its revival in Athens in 1896. The driving force behind the Games' revival, Frenchman Pierre de Coubertin, stated that women were not entitled to compete at the 1896 Summer Olympics because their inclusion would be 'impractical, uninteresting, unaesthetic and incorrect'. This seems to have escaped the attention of the designer of this elegant stamp, which features Pallas Athene, goddess of wisdom, useful arts and prudent warfare.

GREENLAND

**Christian X, decked out in feathers,
Well wrapped up for ghastly weathers.**

Certain stamps strike me as ridiculous: I find this portrait of King Christian X of Denmark, from a set issued in 1938, insufferably pompous. The king, festooned with medals and wearing a silly plumed hat, looks totally incongruous in this artist's impression of Greenland, designed from the comfort of a Copenhagen studio.

Later issues are spectacularly beautiful.

GRENADA

**Grenada, where they make grenades
(No, hold on – was it lemonades?)**

Grenada, or Isle of Spice, was one of the notorious sugar islands, whose prosperity depended on huge numbers of slaves. A Cuban-supported coup in 1983 was quickly overthrown by US Marines in one of their first sorties following the Vietnam debacle. This delightful 1938 monochrome stamp features King George VI festooned with local foliage.

GUATEMALA

**Faded colour, Amerindian,
Pickwick paper, quite Pecksniffian.**

The modern states of El Salvador, Honduras, Nicaragua and Costa Rica were all provinces under Guatemala's jurisdiction in colonial times.

Amerindian culture predominates in Guatemala in a way not seen in other Central American countries, so it was fitting that this early 1878 issue pay tribute to its existence.

GUERNSEY

Henry V and Guernsey Lily:
Island yes, but not of Scilly.

Guernsey received a pounding at the beginning of the German invasion of France in 1940, since the Luftwaffe had not realised that the Channel Islands had been demilitarised some time before; in one incident, lorries about to export tomatoes from St Peter Port to Britain were mistaken for troop transport and bombed. The islands were considered of no value to Germany, but the temptation to occupy part of the British Empire proved too strong. While life under occupation was perhaps less harsh than in continental Europe, some resisted; thus, we read that Guernsey man Percy Miller was sentenced to fifteen months in prison for 'radio offences' and died in Frankfurt.

Here the Guernsey Lily is paired with Henry V, one of the attractive 1969 set.

GUERNSEY (ALDERNEY)

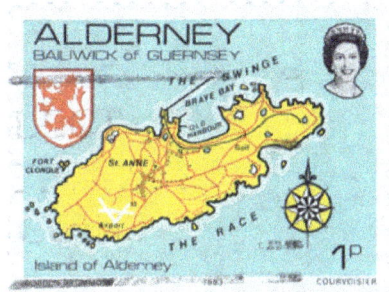

**Alderney, an island map.
Three square miles! I say, old chap!**

During WWII four labour camps were built on Alderney and named after German Frisian islands. Over 700 internees died there.

Given Alderney's tiny size, its claim to postal independence is stretching it a bit, in my opinion – why not use the stamps of Guernsey?

This quite attractive stamp is from the first set issued. The Queen looks very happy.

GUINEA

**A president, a map, a dove:
Guinea is a place I love.**

I remember my mystification at the fact that my artist mother was paid in guineas, a mythical currency still used for purchases of art, horses and bespoke tailoring. However, the guinea coin did once exist.

The Portuguese were active slave traders; later, Guinea, as the French protectorate of Les Rivières du Sud, was detached from Senegal. Sekou Touré, who led the country into independence, flirted with the Soviet Union and China and generally mismanaged the economy (notwithstanding Guinea's huge bauxite reserves) while becoming increasingly severe in his treatment of political opponents. He looks friendly enough on this stamp, one of the first set issued in 1959 to celebrate the country's independence.

GUINEA-BISSAU

**Guinea-Bissau, what a thrill!
Free at last, quite fits the bill.**

'The struggle for dominance around [the Portuguese colony of] Guinea-Bissau fell within the context of the greater scramble for Africa ... which saw English demands for Guinean territories to the south and French demands along the north and east. The Guinean people were certainly not consulted about such matters, and they resisted, revolted, and mutinied by any available means whenever possible... The killings and severe punitive measures exacted by the Portuguese and their mercenaries brought a widespread outcry. Nevertheless, the Portuguese continued their pacification efforts against the Guinean population ... the last of which was undertaken in January 1936.' *(Encyclopaedia Britannica)*

GUYANA

**Bauxite mine, Queen in attendance:
Portrait gone now – independence.**

Britain suffered the humiliation of seeing the terms of its withdrawal from its only colony in South America dictated by the US, who, fearing the left-leaning Premier Cheddi Jagan, delayed independence until the 'right' election results were obtained. Despite having many natural resources, Guyana (the only English-speaking country in South America) remained poor until 2015, when massive offshore oil reserves were discovered.

Guyana was possibly the worst offender when it came to promiscuous stamp production – at one time it seemed as if new issues appeared every ten days.

Miraculously, the overprint has not destroyed the integrity of this fine stamp.

GWALIOR

**Once a state in Central India –
If you're into quiz-like trivia.**

Gwalior is a city in the central Indian state of Madhya Pradesh and was a convention state in the Raj, giving it the 'privilege' of issuing stamps with the portrait of the monarch. This one, in addition to being graced with a splodgy postmark, is stained red at the edges – rust, or strawberry jam courtesy of the Raj? Be that as it may, the Gwalior Fort is surely one of those places to see before you die.

HAITI

**Lefty loosey,
Haighty-taighty.**

Haiti's population is descended almost entirely from African slaves. It gained independence as early as 1804, barely twenty-five years after American independence; its successful Slaves' Revolt sent shivers of apprehension throughout civilised society. Land clearance took place on a massive scale with a view to sugar production, leading to soil erosion. Plagued by civil wars almost as soon as independence was declared, Haiti has never attained any semblance of economic stability.

This 1924 stamp features Christophe's Citadel. Commissioned in 1805 by Henri Christophe and completed in 1820, the fortress was built as part of a system of fortifications designed to thwart potential foreign incursions, notably French.

HATAY

**In Hatay no sushi,
Nor satay that's juicy.**

HATAY DEVLETİ means 'State of Hatay'. Hatay, or modern-day Antalya, was claimed by Italy in 1917 as part of the post-war division of the Ottoman Empire. Arriving in 1919, Italian troops were driven out a mere two years later as part of Kemal Atatürk's nation-building drive.

This is a good example of a postage stamp, or rather its overprint, stating a territorial claim in no uncertain terms. The disfiguring surcharge on this Turkish stamp makes it look as if someone definitely didn't want you to see its original value.

HAWAII

**Charming scene in sepia brown,
Boats off Honolulu Town.**

Mark Twain characterised Hawaii as 'the loveliest fleet of islands that lies anchored in any ocean'. Strong-arm tactics on the part of the US led to the disintegration of the long-standing Hawaiian ruling family's power, and the islands were annexed as a US territory by President McKinley in 1900, achieving full statehood in 1959.

This stamp, dating from 1894, has always charmed me: the frame's tonal gradations are particularly successful, and quite avant-garde for the period.

HONDURAS

**Tegucigalpa, hard to say:
There has to be a simpler way.**

Deadly dull stamp design seems endemic in early Latin American issues, and this Honduran stamp is no exception: over-ornate scrollwork, stubby Wild West lettering. Which is a pity, because President Francisco Morazán was something of a hero: an outstanding military and political leader, elected president of the Federal Republic of Central America in 1830. He introduced many reforms designed to limit the power of the Roman Catholic Church, but his administration aroused the anger of conservatives, whose rebel army defeated him at Guatemala City in 1840. In 1842 he attempted to restore the Federation; he attacked and defeated the forces of the Costa Rican dictator Braulio Carillo, but was eventually betrayed, captured and executed.

HONGKONG

**Queen Victoria green, ten cents,
Never cottoned on to pence.**
'The last stronghold of feudal luxury in the world'.
(Ian Fleming)

Among the most disgraceful episodes of British colonial history must figure the Opium Wars. China, concerned at the amount of Indian-grown opium flowing into Hong Kong through British hands, took action to destroy supplies; at the end of the ensuing conflict, which China lost, Hong Kong was ceded to Britain for a period of ninety-nine years.

Note the stylised frame, a clever reference to ideas we may cherish about Asian art, hidden somewhere in the corners of the mind.

HYDERABAD

**Hyderabad,
There's a good lad.**

Hyderabad is a city in Telangana State, south-central India, just south of the Deccan Plateau. It was particularly badly hit by Hindu-Muslim violence following Indian independence.

The Charminar, a mosque dating from the sixteenth century, is truly breath-taking. Hyderabad's stamps, on the other hand, are anything but, if this poorly engraved 1934 example is anything to go by.

ICELAND

**Iceland:
Niceland.**

Apart from the first reassuringly expensive issues (Danish stamps, cloned), Icelandic stamps are invariably attractive: the modern issues resplendent with colour, and the earlier ones (such as this dramatic 1948 issue commemorating the Hekla eruption of 1947) relying on superior engraving to liven up a monochrome treatment.

INDIA

**Victory Tower, Chittorgarh:
Very big place, Indiarh.**

India's prolific issuing rate doesn't seem to affect its stamp design, which is usually of a high quality. Pre-independence issues are generally (and unusually) dull. This is one of an early post-independence set dating from 1949 which sets the tone for future issues, namely an interest in Indian culture, which had been brushed aside by the stamps of British India. Modern Indian stamps frequently pay tribute to key figures in the literary and scientific world.

No stamp can do credit to the sumptuous decor of the Chittor Fort, built by the Mauryans in the seventh century.

INDONESIA

**Kant wrote *The Critique of Reason*
In classic Indonesian.**

The archipelago of Indonesia stretches one-eighth of the circumference of the world, and has the fourth largest population. The Dutch granted independence to its former colony of the Dutch East Indies in 1949, but only after a protracted four-year conflict (one of the bloodiest of all disengagement struggles), which included the Battle of Surabaya (involving British troops) and the Maidiun Affair, a communist revolt. Thousands died, mostly native Indonesians. Many more died in anti-communist purges in the 1960s.

Indonesia's stamps are generally well designed and cheerfully coloured, akin to the issues of Sri Lanka. This 1960 issue based around agricultural products features the *kelapa* or coconut tree. Despite being monochrome it exudes exuberance.

INDORE

**Wretched Covid, such a bore:
All activities now indore.**

Indore is the largest city in the Indian state of Madhya Pradesh, tracing its roots back to the sixteenth century. It was accorded the privilege of a nineteen-gun salute (makes more noise than an eleven-gun salute) by the Raj, which for reasons beyond my understanding was considered a great honour. Indore has been ranked as India's cleanest city for four years in a row.

This 1928 stamp features the sanguine Yashwant Rao II Holkar XIV ('just call me Rao').

IRAN

**Cyrus, Persia, Nasred-Din:
Can't say that I've ever bin.**

The cruelty of the Iranian regime seems not to weigh in the argument supporting the outside world's restoration of economic ties with Iran. However, the People's Mujahedin of Iran, a powerful democratic movement for regime change led by Maryam Rajavi, is gathering strength.

Iran's post-Islamic Revolution issues feature a fair few beturbanned gents, as well as others of a militaristic nature. No butterflies, thankfully. This 1891 stamp, somewhat the worse for wear, sports the legend POSTE PERSANE. It harks from a different era altogether: Nasred-Din was the first Persian ruler to be made a Knight of the Order of the Garter, and also the first to be photographed.

IRAQ

**Iran, Iraq, a bloody war
That through the Indus Valley tore.**

This elegant, winged cherub, part of a set issued in 1923, is a reminder of just how glorious was Mesopotamian culture, easily forgotten in the light of the horrors of the Iran-Iraq war, Saddam's invasion of Kuwait and George Bush Senior's bombing of Baghdad.

Note the inscriptions in both Arabic and English.

IRELAND

**Methinks this reaper not so grim –
Perchance 'tis but the artist's whim.**

For my native country I have chosen this elegant stamp commemorating the bicentenary of the foundation of the Royal Dublin Society in 1731. Known internationally for its hosting of the Dublin Horse Show, the 'RDS', along with a handful of other Irish institutions, has kept the word 'Royal' in its title.

There is much to admire in this stamp, notably the elegantly drawn reaper (observe the confident gait and the relaxed posture of the arms) as well as the older, handsome Gaelic alphabet, whose demise I lament. It bore a certain resemblance to the German *Sütterlin* script.

ISLE OF MAN

**Lump of earth in Irish Sea,
Celtic tale and pedigree.**

Created from a clod of earth hurled into the Irish Sea by Fionn Mac Cumhaill, the Isle of Man has had a separate postal administration since 1973. Its stamps are as dull as its fiscal practice is dubious (ranked seventeenth in a list of sixty-four different jurisdictions*) but the landscape is reassuringly similar to County Wicklow, as J.H. Nicholson's attractive 1977 *View from Ramsey* shows. I have happy memories of performing Don Alfonso in *Così fan tutte* in Port St Mary as a student.

Manx kippers are second to none.

*Tax Justice Network, 2019

IVORY COAST

**Boatloads of ivory,
Awful connivery.**

France claimed Ivory Coast as a colony in 1893 (quite why the country has not changed its name given the appalling life of ivory porters is a mystery). Louis Léon César Faidherbe, featured here, takes posthumous pride of place in this 1906 landscape of palms and a suspension bridge. Faidherbe, a military hero and one of the few competent generals of the disastrous Franco-Prussian War, was determined to implement the 'Plan of 1854', intended to consolidate gains in French West Africa. He even dreamed of the French Empire being extended from Senegal to the Red Sea.

JAIPUR

**Jaipur this and Jaipur that,
Rajasthani tit-for-tat.**

Rajasthan's capital city, Jaipur, boasts the Hawa Mahal ('Hall of Winds'), high up on my list of must-see places. Jaipur, briefly independent from 1947 to 1949, was one of the feudatory states. This 1931 stamp features a confident Maharaja Sawai Man Singh II (1912—1970), who, in addition to his polo-playing skills, did much to modernise Jaipur, so much so that it was chosen to be the capital of Rajasthan. He was the last of Jaipur's maharajas.

JAMAICA

**Make a breaka
For Jamaica.**

The frame of this attractive 1938 stamp inscribed 'Bamboo Walk' seems to be constructed out of bamboo, aptly enough. Jamaica was the first British colony to establish a post office (as early as 1671), but during the eighteenth-century local planters preferred to entrust their mail to merchant ship captains rather than the postmaster, one Edward Dismore, who they claimed charged exorbitant fees. Inter-island post was for many years a sorry affair: a letter sent from Jamaica to Barbados, for instance, having to pass through either Halifax, New York or London.

More recent Jamaican stamps are mostly humdrum affairs.

JAPAN

**It's rather long from head to toe,
This lovely archipelago.**

According to the *Encyclopaedia Britannica,* 'Tension between old and new is apparent in all phases of Japanese life. A characteristic sensitivity to natural beauty and a concern with form and balance are evident in such cities as Kyōto and Nara, as well as in Japan's ubiquitous gardens. Even in the countryside, however, the impact of rapid Westernisation is evident in many aspects of Japanese life. The agricultural regions are characterized by low population densities and well-ordered rice fields and fruit orchards, whereas the industrial and urbanized belt along the Pacific coast of Honshu is noted for its highly concentrated population, heavy industrialisation, and environmental pollution.'

Post-war Japanese stamps are some of the most beautiful ever issued.

JERSEY

**Only those who feel they're worthy
Dare to buy a house in Jersey.**

Jersey's post-war reputation has been tarnished by stories of collaboration during WWII. This has been bitterly disputed, and indeed insult was added to injury by the British government's refusal to acknowledge Norman Lebrocq, the leader of Jersey's resistance, whereas some collaborators were awarded knighthoods and OBEs.

Jersey's stamps are cheerfully dull, but this one, one of the first sets issued under the Independent Postal Administration in 1969, is an exception: an effort has been made to incorporate elements of Jersey's marine life into the frame, in this case *vraic*, a seaweed used as fertiliser.

JIND

**I wouldn't mind
A jind and tonic.**

One of India's convention states, now in the state of Haryana in north-west India. Its earliest stamps are rather attractive, but all other issues are simply British Indian stamps overprinted JIND STATE. This stamp's design – to my eye at least – seems somewhat overloaded, although it won the approval of George V, himself a keen stamp collector.

JOHORE

**'Johore,' they said, so off I went;
Had fun galore, from heaven sent.**

Johore was the southernmost state of the Federation of Malaya, incorporated into Malaysia in 1963. The governors of the Johore Sultanate were recognised as independent by the British in the Cession of Singapore (1819).

I used to puzzle about the unhappy sitter for this portrait, and in fact Sultan Sir Ibrahim (1873—1959) was deeply unpopular, owing to his opposition to Malayan independence. The glasses don't help. On the other hand, he was fabulously wealthy.

JORDAN

**O river most biblical,
Your water's equivocal.**

If you have it, flaunt it: the extraordinary El-Deir Temple in Petra (technically speaking sculpture, not architecture) is featured on this ornate 1954 stamp. The Hashemite royal family of Jordan have ruled the country since 1921; at that time, they also briefly ruled Syria, Iraq and parts of Saudi Arabia (the Hejaz) as a reward for their alliance with Britain during WWI. Jordan lost a significant swathe of its territory to Israel during the third Arab-Israeli war in 1967, notably Bethlehem, Hebron, Jericho, Nablus, Ramallah, Janīn and the city of Jerusalem. In 1988 Jordan renounced its claims to these areas.

KATANGA

**Lumumba's torture, '61,
Tyrant's victory, quickly won.**

Katanga, the richest of Congo's provinces, was the scene of great strife following independence. In 1960, led by a local politician, Moise Tshombe, and supported by foreign mining interests, Katanga seceded from the newly independent Congo, provoking a period of civil unrest and bloodshed in which it was opposed by UN and Congolese forces. It was gradually reintegrated into Congo.

The short-lived political changes are adroitly incorporated into the stamp's overprint.

KAZAKHSTAN

**Kazakhstan is large and sweetish,
Full of hamsters and quite cheapish.**

Nursultan Nazarbayev has dominated much of Kazakhstan's post-Soviet history; his strong-arm tactics towards striking oil workers in the town of Zhanaozen in May 2011 led to seventeen being killed.

A little of the gaudiness of late Soviet stamps is evident in Kazakh issues, but the butterfly trap is avoided, and the number of portraits of historical figures featured on its stamps augurs well for the future.

Considering its enormous size (Kazakhstan is the ninth largest country in the world) there is something amusing about this tiny stamp.

KEDAH

**Sheaf of rice, the 2c green
Paints an oriental scene.**

Somewhat marred by the domineering postmark, this handsome stamp featuring a sheaf of rice was part of the first set issued by Kedah in 1912. Kedah, one of the Malaysian states, was tossed around like an old pillow: it was invaded by Malacca, Portugal, Aceh and Siam in turn, until its transfer to Britain under the terms of the Anglo-Siamese Treaty of 1909. It joined (reluctantly) the Malayan Federation in 1948.

The Hanging Bridge with Cable Car at Langkawi looks like a lot of fun, while the Masjid Zahir Mosque in Alor Setar, built in 1912, has been voted one of the top ten most beautiful mosques in the world.

KELANTAN

**Yet another eastern enclave:
Went there once and had a close shave.**

Just down the road from Kedah, Kelantan is another of the thirteen Malaysian states. There must have been tacit complicity between these states when it came to stamp design, since many of them are identical.

Owing to Kelantan's rural location and culture, Kelantanese Malay is unintelligible to some Malays. Kelantan is known for *wau bulan* (kite-flying), *gasing* (top-spinning) and *silat* (martial arts).

Here, a jaded-looking Sultan Ibrahim looks as if a spell working in the pineapple fields would have done him the world of good.

KENYA

**Independent state, wood carving:
Hope the artist wasn't starving.**

Even a potted history of Kenya would take up pages: its role in WWI alone, where thousands were forced to serve as soldiers and porters, often dying of disease; the brutal suppression of the Mau-Mau revolt after WWII, one of the worst of the British disentanglements, and, of course, the colour bar.

On the whole Kenya lives up to the promise of its first issues: colourful, but with a sophistication often absent in those of its neighbours. This attractive monochrome stamp featuring a woodcarver is part of the first set of Kenyan stamps, issued in 1963. *Uhuru* means freedom in Swahili; Kenya's first president was named Uhuru Kenyatta.

KENYA, UGANDA & TANGANYIKA

**Muted colours, Lake Naivasha,
King looks on, an English pasha.**

At the beginning of Edward VII's reign Britain possessed fifteen out of the thirty colonies and protectorates in Africa, as well as the profits accruing from them: these included coffee from Uganda, tea from Kenya and gold, diamonds and a host of other minerals from Tanganyika.

When it came to stamp design, Britain often paid more than lip service to the land it occupied: this handsome stamp, part of a 1938 set, is one of the best examples. The French often contented themselves with reproducing the same image multiple times, simply changing the colour scheme; Portugal stayed true to her corpulent, moody Ceres, and Germany was happy to sail around in the imperial yacht.

KIAUTSCHOU

**Leased by Germany from China,
Ended up in Carolina.**

And speaking of imperial yachts, this is one of the higher values in the *Hohenzollern* series, and rather more imposing to boot (note the currency: dollars). Kiautschou was not a colony as such, but was leased by China to Germany from 1898 to 1914. As it was initially intended as a coaling station for its rapidly expanding fleet, Germany invested huge sums in Kiautschou. The impoverished fishing village of Tsingtao, for instance, was laid out with wide streets, modern housing, electrification throughout, a sewer system and a safe drinking water supply, a rarity in much of Asia at that time. Germany was forced to relinquish its leasehold by Japan in 1914 (Japan having sided with the Allies in WWI).

KIRIBATI

**Gilbert Islands once they were,
Change of name, a brief transfer.**

Formerly the Gilbert Islands (q.v.), the thirty-three islands of Kiribati (pronounced 'Kiribass*)* are scattered over a vast area of ocean. The name Kiribati is a patois rendition of 'Gilberts'. In common with other islands in the Pacific Ocean, Kiribati's very existence is threatened by rising sea levels: in 2014 it purchased eight square miles of Fijian territory 'in case'.

This 2002 stamp, one of a set of tropical fish, is a real eye-catcher. No postmark, my apologies.

KOREA

**Long before the parallel,
Peaceful country, doing well.**

Korea was formerly an empire under Chinese suzerainty, before being annexed by Japan in 1910. This rather lovely 1903 stamp, complete with Art Nouveau floral design, bears the legend POSTES IMPÉRIALES DE CORÉE. We have encountered the same linguistic phenomenon in the case of the Baghdad and Persian stamps seen earlier; presumably it was thought that French would impart a certain chic to the stamp.

KUWAIT

**Cruel invasion, First Gulf War,
Dodgy neighbour right next door.**

Having just watched a promotional video about Kuwait City, I think it is safe to say that it is very flat and very modern (none of its buildings seem to be more than twenty years old), and includes some rather beautiful skyscrapers.

Wara Hill is a landmark in a country that is mostly flat. Later Kuwaiti issues share many of the characteristics of Middle Eastern stamps in general: colourful but occasionally overcrowded. This 1961 stamp is one of only a handful of line-engraved issues.

KYRGYZSTAN

**Kyrgyzstan, a rugged land:
Mountains, lakes and even quicksand.**

Mostly mountainous (in fact, a mountaineer's dream), the former Soviet republic of Kyrgyzstan declared independence in 1991. The country lurches between civil unrest and authoritarian crackdowns, the most serious taking place in 2010 in the capital, Bishkek, when an attempt to overthrow the government of Kurmanbek Bakiyev resulted in eighty deaths. Tensions also exist between the Kyrgyz majority and the Uzbek minority.

Stamp design is generally pleasing. I have a soft spot for stamps that clearly show the date of issue, such as this one. Cataloguing Swedish stamps, for instance, is a nightmare – for the opposite reason.

LAOS

**More bombs fell on Laos in the Vietnam War
Than fell on its neighbour, right next door.**

The Geneva Accords of 1954 marked the end of French rule in South East Asia. Laos was plagued by civil war (1959–75), during which the US and North Vietnam fought a proxy war there (the 'Secret War'). It is estimated that more bombs were dropped on Laos than on Vietnam itself during the Vietnam conflict.

This remarkably ugly stamp (attractive colours notwithstanding) reflects the bellicosity of the period (1968). Earlier Laotian issues are very beautiful, particularly those of the 1950s. Stamp design went through a bad patch in the 1980s, but has rallied in recent years.

LATVIA

**Latvia, wee nation state,
Punches well above its weight.**

This stamp, featuring the Ruins of Rezekne, is one of a set issued in 1928 to commemorate ten years of Latvian independence. Latvia's history is one of the most complex I have ever read: tossed about between greater and lesser powers such as Germany, Poland and Lithuania, it faced its biggest challenge during Soviet rule, when increasing russification threatened its very existence; there are still occasional spats with Russia over Latvia's treatment of the Russian minority.

Early issues such as this one are idiosyncratic and generally pleasing. Post-Soviet issues are quite simply stunning.

LEBANON

**Lofty cedars, ancient stones,
History filling many tomes.**

Legendary for its cuisine and (sadly) for what seemed like its interminable civil war, Lebanon, whose economic meltdown was recently compounded by the dreadful warehouse explosion in Beirut, suffered from years of Ottoman and French Mandate rule. Its stamps, however, are up there with the best of the Middle Eastern issues, such as this one, from a set of birds (and butterflies) issued in 1965. This is the Northern Bullfinch.

LEEWARD ISLANDS

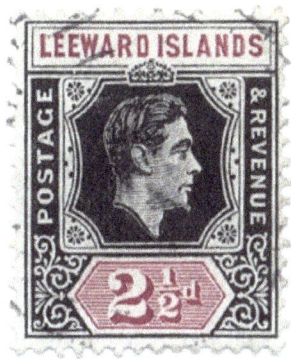

**Slaves that from their homes were sundered,
Working fields that had been plundered.**

The British Leeward Islands – Antigua, Dominica, Montserrat, Nevis, St Christopher (St Kitts) and the Virgin Islands – all used postage stamps inscribed LEEWARD ISLANDS between 1890 and 1956, often concurrently with stamps inscribed with the individual colony's name. Post-1956 no more stamps were issued for the Leeward Islands, meaning that we are spared the fawning portraits of members of the Royal Family that adorn so many modern Caribbean issues. This sober/flamboyant stamp issued in 1938 is as good as it gets – there are no pictorial issues.

LESOTHO

**In what was once Basutoland,
This sorghum needs a loving hand.**

Historically and economically stuck between a rock and a hard place owing to its being encircled by South Africa, Lesotho, despite being dubbed a Fourth World country, also possesses some of the world's most spectacular topography: it is the only country in the world to be entirely above 1,000m in elevation, and has the highest lowest point in the entire world at 1,400m. Lesotho also boasts 300 days of sunshine annually. However, its stamps (apart from this attractively spartan issue from 1971) are fairly awful, being produced as a cash crop to satisfy the whims of an undiscriminating philatelic clientele.

LIBERIA

**Freedom's beacon, stars and stripes,
Has its share of modern gripes.**

Liberia was established on land acquired in 1821 by the American Colonization Society for freed US slaves. Liberian independence was proclaimed in 1847 and its boundaries expanded. The country enjoyed relative stability until the destructive civil war of the 1990s which dragged on until 2003.

Issues up to the end of WWII are mostly well designed and occasionally very attractive; thereafter it's rapidly downhill. This starkly ugly stamp (designed on the occasion of a philatelic exhibition!) shares certain characteristics with Brazilian issues from the same period (1956).

LIBYA

**Romans first, Italians later,
Giant sand dunes, quite first-rater.**

If the early years of Italian colonisation in Africa were generally benign, from the 1930s onwards the situation changed drastically. Italy committed major war crimes during WWII, such as refusing to take prisoners of war and instead executing surrendering combatants and civilians (including children), in addition to bombing tribal villages with mustard gas. Italy also committed ethnic cleansing by expelling 100,000 Bedouin Cyrenaicans, almost half the population of Cyrenaica, from their settlements. Most of these atrocities took place in what is now Libya.

This high value stamp was used on a registered envelope, as can be seen from the postmark.

LIECHTENSTEIN

© Liechtenstein

**Landlocked little principality,
Vaduz its municipality.**

This tiny principality is beloved of stamp collectors: it takes on many positive characteristics of Swiss stamp design, while avoiding the philatelic pitfalls of its other neighbour, Austria. Its banking sector was recently reformed as a result of tax scrutiny by the US and EU, a case of pots calling kettles black. It is the world's leading producer of … false teeth.

This beautiful 1930 stamp features the 'Drei Schwestern', and incorporates a generous sprig of edelweiss into its upper frame.

LITHUANIA

**Without the 'Lith' it's just 'Uania' –
It might as well be Pomerania.**

Lithuania follows the same philatelic pattern as its two Baltic neighbours: a relatively short period of independence featuring colourful, idiosyncratic issues, then incorporation into the USSR, followed by a resurgence of excellent stamp design on re-attaining independence. Stamps such as this 1921 'Sower' are generally concerned with national reconstruction: the same theme crops up in other European countries.

Lithuania's small size belies the fact that it was once a large empire, stretching from the Baltic to the Black Sea and reaching its apogee at the beginning of the fifteenth century.

LOURENÇO MARQUES

All these tiny bits of land!
Postmark smudged: a heavy hand.

According to the dubious tenets of pluricontinentalism (an ugly word used specifically with reference to the Portuguese colonies), Portugal was not an empire as such, but rather a unitary nation state dispersed across South America (Brazil), Africa (Angola and Mozambique) and Asia (Goa). Lourenço Marques, named after the explorer, became modern-day Maputo, capital of Mozambique. Here, again, we have a well-fed Ceres, standard issue for all the Portuguese colonies, and as dull as they come. Did she approve, one wonders, of the 'Education through Work' colonial policy (a euphemism for forced labour) espoused by Lisbon?

LUXEMBOURG

**Rocky fells and winding rivers,
Tax-free booze: not good for livers.**

The name Luxembourg derives from the Saxon *Lucilinburhuc,* meaning 'little fortress', and indeed the number of castles in this small country bears witness to Luxembourg's past need to defend itself against bigger neighbours. It was passed around between Spain, the Habsburgs and France for several centuries, before being eventually annexed to the Netherlands at the Congress of Vienna in 1815, as a personal possession (Grand Duchy) of the Dutch monarch, gaining full independence on the dissolution of the German Confederation in 1866.

Some of the early issues, including this 1935 view of Vianden, are beautiful, but later ones are often simply dull.

MACAO

In former times casinos thrived;
I wonder, have they still survived?

Macao is a small peninsula at the mouth of the Canton River, now part of the Chinese province of Guangdong. The first Portuguese arrived in 1513, but not until 1951 did Macao officially become a part of Portugal. It was returned to China in 1999. In terms of economic success, Macao never came close to its near neighbour Hong Kong, but made up the shortfall partly through casino revenues.

Macao's stamps are carbon copies of Portugal's; after the handover to China in 1999 there is a palpable improvement in design. This 1956 stamp would have been useful for map reading were it not for the postmark.

MADAGASCAR

**This giant island boasts lemurs,
Huge baobabs and native cures.**

On independence in 1958 Madagascar became the Malagasy Republic but reverted to the name Madagascar in 1992. It was declared a French colony in 1898. A full-scale insurrection against French rule in 1947 left an estimated 11,000 natives dead; thousands more are thought to have died from famine and cold. A close inspection of this 1908 stamp may reveal a clue as to why the French were not popular: luckless natives haul a lazy colonist up a steep slope near Antananarivo. My catalogue describes the stamp, with unwitting facetiousness, as 'Transport in Madagascar'.

MADEIRA

**Imagine Italy without the lira,
Or life, indeed, without Madeira!**

Madeira is a hillwalker's paradise, also known for its eponymous wine. It was first colonised in 1420 by the Portuguese, who found the islands uninhabited.

The Legend of Machico, featured on this 1997 stamp, is a sad tale about two luckless English lovers at the time of the Hundred Years War who eloped and became stranded on Madeira. The young lady died from the ill effects of a stormy crossing; the young man, Machim, erected a large cross in her memory, before succumbing to melancholy a week later. The stylised rendition is rather touching.

MALACCA

**Lots of places like Malacca
Were addicted to tobacca.**

Malacca (now Melaka), one of the Malaysian states, was once an important trading hub and as such was fought over by the Chinese, Vietnamese, Dutch and Portuguese, before ending up a British possession until its incorporation into Malaysia in 1963.

The Seri Negeri Complex, housing the state government administrative offices, is a remarkable piece of architecture, well worth a detour. As for this 1954 stamp, the palm trees and decorated frame seem to reflect a certain end-of-empire listlessness.

MALAGASY REPUBLIC

**How confusing, changing names –
Better if they stays the sames.**

There's only so much a stamp designer can do when presented with a commission to depict this very dull bridge spanning the River Sofia. Philibert Tsiranana (1912—1978), after whom the bridge was named, was the first president of the Malagasy Republic. Despite a penchant for authoritarianism, he was generally admired.

MALAYAN FEDERATION

Tedious, these federations,
Made up of all sorts of nations.

The road to full statehood for Malaysia was long but generally speaking peaceful. The Malayan Federation, an independent country within the British Commonwealth, existed from 1957 until its dissolution in 1963, at which point the modern state of Malaysia came into being. This not unattractive 1957 stamp serves as a useful map for the Malay States. Note the Malacca postmark.

MALAYSIA

**My dearest fantasia:
To live in Malaysia.**

As luck would have it, this attractive issue is Malaysia's first: one can clearly see the 'Swiss cheese' effect of Brunei (which chose not to join the Federation) tucked away between Sabah and Sarawak on the island of Borneo), as well as Singapore, which declared independence in 1965. 'Singapore had seceded from Malaysia in 1965 (at the invitation of the Malaysian government) because of political friction between the state and central governments. That conflict had ethnic overtones.' (*Encyclopaedia Britannica*). Note the country name in English only, not in Arabic and English as in the previous stamp.

MALDIVES

**A chunky building, quite a spadeful,
Five times a day it calls the faithful.**

Ruled by the Portuguese, Dutch and British in turn, the Maldives became independent in 1952. None of the 200 or so inhabited islands of the archipelago rise to more than six feet above sea level.

As far as stamps go, anything up to the mid-1960s is decent enough; thereafter it's downhill all the way, courtesy of the butterfly trap. This 1909 stamp contrives to be simply dull, which is strange, because in real life the minaret of the Old Friday Mosque in Malé is striking enough.

MALI

**Checked in for a morning flight to Bali,
And found myself exploring Mali.**

Mali owes its existence to the break-up of the Federation of French Sudan and Senegal, which had formed an autonomous republic within the French-African community in 1959. In 1960 the French-Sudanese half became Mali. Most of its post-colonial history has been blighted by coups, border disputes with Burkina Faso, insurgencies by Tuaregs and Islamists, desertification, drought and a weak economy.

Stamp design, initially very French in style (with all that that implies), has in the last two decades descended into a philatelic bargain basement.

MALTA

**WWII was not a breeze:
Plucky people, the Maltese.**

In recognition of its bravery in the face of fierce German offensives, the George Cross (pictured above) was awarded to the entire population of Malta in 1942. Self-government was granted in 1947, revoked in 1959, and then restored in 1962 (which sounds odd).

There's a little too much of the Channel Islands in Maltese stamp design to please me, but Malta remains very popular with collectors. The George VI issues of 1938 go some way towards redeeming matters.

MANCHUKO

**A puppet regime long ago,
'Tis part of China now, Manchuko.**

The Japanese puppet government of Manchuko (The State of Manchuria) under Emperor Pu Yi was set up in 1932 and lasted until the end of WWII. Japan had been active in the region since its victory in the Russo-Japanese War (1904–05) and regarded Manchuko as being vital to its expansionist plans, brought to fruition following its invasion of the area under the flimsiest of pretexts.

This cheerful 1936 stamp features the Pei Ling Mausoleum, which housed members of the Manchu dynasty.

MARSHALL ISLANDS

**Far away in the Pacific
Children's games are just terrific.**

Named after British naval captain John Marshall (1748—1819), the Marshall Islands comprises no fewer than 1,200 islands, many uninhabited owing to a shortage of water. Nominally independent since 1991, it is largely dependent on the US for economic aid. A missile-testing site provides the main employment for the 56,000 inhabitants.

Early stamps date from the time of the German Protectorate. Contemporary stamp design owes much to the US. This rather vile 1990 stamp features a coconut-palm leaf windmill, which to my Irish eyes looks for all the world like a St Brigid's Cross. The child appears to be on the sunny side of thirty.

MARTINIQUE

**Nor gold nor silver try to seek
If you should go to Martinique.**

The last colonial issues for Martinique, now an overseas French *département,* date from 1947. Some are quite attractive, but this job-lot allegorical affair, which crops up regularly in this book, has tested our patience for the last time.

One of the most densely populated islands of the Antilles, Martinique boasts an active volcano, Mont Pelée; during the deadly eruption of 1902 it claimed 30,000 lives, including that of French-Polish stamp designer Paul Merwart (q.v. French Somali Coast).

MAURITANIA

**Red and brown, a handsome fellow
(Although I much prefer deep yellow).**

Mauritania, largely desert, forms a cultural transition zone between the Arab and Berber peoples in the north and the 'Sudan' people of the south (from the Arabic *Bilād al-Sudān,* 'land of the blacks').

I find it difficult to enthuse about French colonial stamp design in general, but this is one of the better ones (q.v. Ivory Coast). We have already encountered the figure of Faidherbe, Governor of French Senegal, who adorns many French colonial stamps; he was the architect of French colonial expansion in the nineteenth century and proponent of the 'Plan of 1854'. Faidherbe was something of a rarity in that he did not espouse the anti-Muslim views of his day.

MAURITIUS

**To die in Mauritius –
Now, that were propitious!**

Stamp collectors are strange people: it's enough for a stamp to be very rare to get philatelic hearts racing. Aesthetical questions do not really weigh in the balance; if they did, the crudely designed but extremely valuable first stamps of Mauritius would be less sought-after. Having reached this point in the book, you will have realised that my philatelic predilections point in the direction of the School of Fine Arts.

There is a certain homemade charm about early Mauritian stamps, but later issues disappoint. This 1989 view of *Le Morne* is spectacular kitsch.

MEMEL

**German once, now Lithuanian,
Baltic Sea, Episcopalian.**

This is the story of a disconsolate 1920 French lassie overprinted in German. Before WWI Memelland, a region bordering the Baltic Sea, belonged to Prussia. A large portion of its population, however, was Lithuanian, and after the war the newly formed state of Lithuania requested that the Allied Powers grant it possession of the Memel territory. The Allied Powers did detach Memelland from Germany, but rather than annex the region to Lithuania, whose political situation was at that time unstable, they assumed direct control over the area, appointing a French administration. This irked the Lithuanians, who eventually had *gain de cause* in 1923. Memel was renamed Klaipėda, an autonomous region within Lithuania.

MEXICO

**Cactus-filled and rather sandy,
Hemmed in by the Rio Grande.**

In terms of stamp design, Mexico gets off to a shaky start: the usual sombre portraits and overcrowded 'Buffalo Bill' type stamps are typical of design up until the 1920s. Thereafter things improve rapidly, and contemporary Mexican design can hold its own with the best of the Europeans. This 1937 airmail stamp, although lacking finesse in terms of execution, at least gives us a flavour of the country.

MOLDOVA

**O, let the Bessarabian deportations
A warning be to all ye nations!**

I lazily assumed, looking at this stamp, that it commemorated the victims of Nazi atrocity; in fact, the dates tell us that it commemorates the Bessarabian deportation. On 12–13 June 1941, almost 30,000 members of families of 'counter-revolutionaries and nationalists' from the Moldavian SSR were deported by Stalin to various destinations in the USSR. It is estimated that in 1940-41 200,000 to 300,000 Romanian Bessarabians were persecuted, conscripted into forced labour camps, or deported, of whom many did not survive.

This design is chillingly effective.

MONACO

**Monaco, a tiny place,
Is dominated by a race.**

Monaco should actually be slightly bigger: under the terms of the Franco-Monegasque Treaty of 1861 it lost the towns of Menton and Roquebrune. Tiny countries usually remain independent because of their impregnable terrain (one thinks of San Marino), and Monaco would have been easily defendable in times past. A brief visit left me with the impression that there is little of architectural interest apart from the Oceanographic Museum, the Casino and the Opera House. Its stamps, including the rather dreary one featured above, are generally speaking carbon copies of French design.

MONGOLIA

**Gobi desert, Genghis Khan,
Doughty warriors to a man.**

Early Mongolian issues up until roughly 1960 are not without interest and make an effort to reflect the culture of the land, after which a kind of poor man's Soviet stamp design is all too evident. Design (though not necessarily choice of subject) shows signs of significant improvement from 2000 or so. This stamp is part of an attractive 1958 animal set.

MONTENEGRO

**Rather small but very scenic,
Though the king looks quite anaemic.**

This 1910 stamp shows King Nicholas I of Montenegro as a young prince in 1855; at the time of its issue he was about seventy years old. Nicholas, Montenegro's only king, was an implacable enemy of the Ottoman Empire, and his military exploits in the Russo-Turkish war of 1877–78 gained considerable territory for Montenegro, even if some of the gains were reduced as a result of the Congress of Berlin in 1878.

This richly decorated, splendidly Art Nouveau stamp is striking. Modern issues are colourful and occasionally very attractive.

MONTSERRAT

**What a lovely, peaceful scene!
Nice engraving, all in green.**

Known as the Emerald Isle of the Caribbean, Montserrat was named after the eponymous Spanish religious site and was colonised by Irish Catholics under the aegis of the governor of St Kitts. It was christened 'Land of the prickly bush' by the first Indian settlers. More than half of Montserrat was placed in an exclusion zone following the 1995 volcanic eruption.

Most British colonial issues from the watershed year of 1938 are bicoloured, but this monochrome scene is a delight: the stylised foliage draped around the '½d.' is particularly effective, as is the coat of arms, in which a lassie representing 'Erin' holds on for dear life to cross and harp.

MOROCCO

You must remember this:
A kiss is just a kiss.

This splendid painting, entitled *Spahi Horsemen*, is by Moroccan artist Hassan el Glaoui (1924—2018). The Spahis were cavalry regiments of the French army recruited primarily from the indigenous populations of Algeria, Tunisia and Morocco. The modern French Army retains one regiment of Spahis as an armoured unit, with personnel now recruited in mainland France.

MOROCCO AGENCIES

**A trowel, a dove, a nice brick wall:
Morocco made to feel quite small.**

The British post offices in Morocco, also known as the 'Morocco Agencies', were a system of post offices operated by Gibraltar and later the United Kingdom. Morocco Agencies' stamps, apart from those of Tangier, were issued in three currencies. The offices were closed following Moroccan independence in 1957.

This stamp is from the attractive British 'Victory' set issued in 1946.

MOZAMBIQUE

**Meekly led unto the slaughter,
Mozambiquely on the altar.**

It's good to see a poet rather than a head of state being honoured on a stamp having wide circulation. The sixteenth-century Portuguese poet Luís de Camões is reckoned to be his country's finest. *Os Lusíadas* ('The Lusiads') is his best-known work, as shown in a comically oversized edition on this standard-issue colonial stamp. Published in 1572, *Os Lusíadas* is widely regarded as the most important work of Portuguese literature and is frequently compared to Virgil's *Aeneid*. The work celebrates the discovery of a sea route to India by Vasco da Gama.

MOZAMBIQUE COMPANY

Sounds quite harmless as a place;
Now it's fallen quite from grace.

Portugal leased large tracts of land in its colony, Mozambique, to chartered companies, who were permitted to exploit the lands and peoples of specific areas in exchange for an obligation to develop agriculture, communications and social services. The Mozambique Company was established in this manner in the 1890s. However, the plantations depended largely on a conscripted workforce. Folks back home in Lisbon, looking at this attractive 1918 stamp, must have thought it was a lovely place.

MUSCAT & OMAN

**Oh, to be Roman
In Muscat & Oman!**

Now known simply as Oman (q.v.), this Arabian state is a land of topographical contrasts: the interior basically desert, the coast tropical and lush and known especially for its Muscat grapes, thought to be the world's oldest variety. Muscat was overrun at different times by the Portuguese and Persians. A palace coup in 1970 saw Sultan Saʻīd overthrown by his son, Qaboos bin Said. Qaboos quickly reversed his father's policy of isolation and began to develop and modernise Oman. Muscat and Oman's stamp-issuing reign lasted a mere three years; this somewhat dull 1966 stamp features the national coat of arms. Only three sets were ever issued.

NABHA

**One of those convention states,
Or so my catalogue relates.**

As one of the Indian convention states, Nabha State enjoyed the privilege of overprinting British Indian stamps. Nabha was a city state in the Punjab, whose Hira Mahal is a glorious piece of architecture – although the glory is faded. Note how the name NABHA STATE is overprinted, not incorporated into the stamp's design. Stamps from other colonial powers tended to use the same design but at least printed the name of the country in a tablet at the base of the stamp (q.v. Martinique and other early French and Portuguese colonial issues). This stamp was intended for use by the state administration.

NATAL

**This land, whose end was nearly fatal,
Once called itself (I think) Pre-Natal.**

The Afrikaners' establishment of the Republic of Natal was opposed by the British, who annexed the colony in 1843. In response, many of the former republic's Afrikaner inhabitants left for the Transvaal and the Orange Free State and were replaced by new immigrants, mainly from Britain.

Natal was made a crown colony in 1856. Its first stamps are reassuringly expensive; its last were issued in 1908. Although there are no pictorial issues, the King Edward VII set includes many bicoloured stamps, such as this striking example. The blotchy postmark doesn't help.

NAURU

**The coronation of King George VI
Has never made it to Netflix.**

A former German possession, incorporated into the Marshall Islands Protectorate, Nauru passed into Australian hands following WWI. Heavily bombed by the USAF during WWII, it became independent in 1968 – the first of the Micronesian nations to do so. With an area of just eight square miles, it is the smallest island nation in the world; it is also, sadly, the fattest. Phosphate mining formerly provided enormous wealth, but with its disappearance the island suffered economic decline. In 2001 Australia offered money to Nauru in return for accepting Afghan and Iraqi refugees.

NEGRI SEMBILAN

**I think it's such a lovely name:
Obsequious leaders, tigers tame.**

One of the Malayan states, incorporated into Malaysia in 1963, Negri Sembilan means 'nine states'. Rich tin reserves attracted British interest, which offered 'protection' in 1874. Negri Sembilan boasts staggeringly beautiful Minangkabau architecture, often associated with Indonesia. Minangkabau houses reflect their natural environment, in particular the concave roof designs that resemble buffalo horns. Sadly, this beauty did not spill over into Negri Sembilan's stamp design; this one is a carbon copy of that of Malacca (q.v.), with the Queen's head replaced by dreary heraldry.

NEPAL

**Stand tall,
Nepal!**

Nepal expected to become a satellite state within the British Empire, like its much bigger neighbour India, but in fact an accommodation was reached between the ruling Rana family and Britain in the 1860s. In return for providing troops (the famous Gurkhas) and accepting British guidance on matters of foreign policy, Nepal was guaranteed protection from foreign enemies as well as autonomy in domestic affairs.

Nepalese stamps are attractive enough, although generally lacking the finesse of Indian stamp design. Nepal's first issues date from 1881; this 1907 stamp features Shiva Mahadeva, one of the principal Hindu deities.

THE NETHERLANDS

**Golden Age, East Indian, spicy,
Real estate here very pricy.**

Contemporary Dutch stamp design is good enough in its own way, but the most beautiful issues to my mind are those of the interbellum years, coinciding with the Art Deco movement. This 1864 stamp featuring King Willem II wins no prizes for design. Like the first Belgian stamps, it shows no country name, but comically enough bears the legend POSTZEGEL, or 'stamp'.

If you're passing through Utrecht, make a detour to see its stunning Art Deco Post Office.

NETHERLANDS ANTILLES

**This place was really very far
For your Netherlandish tar.**

The Netherlands Antilles comprises five islands: Sint Eustatius, Saba and Sint Maarten forming one group, and a second group comprising Curaçao and Bonaire, both situated near Venezuela. They formed an integral part of the Netherlands, with full autonomy, but in 2010 Curaçao and Sint Maarten became autonomous countries within the kingdom, a status similar to that of Aruba. Bonaire, Saba and Sint Eustatius became special municipalities with closer ties to central government. Sint Maarten shares its island with Saint-Martin, a French Overseas Collectivity.

NETHERLANDS INDIES

**Java, Bali, other places,
Sun-kissed, ruled by other races.**

Most of the Netherlands Indies (or Dutch East Indies) became part of an independent Indonesia from 1949. Under Dutch rule land-grabbing, spurred on by the idea of immense financial gains, continued almost unabated until 1920.

The Dutch believed they had a moral duty to free the native Indonesian peoples from indigenous rulers who were considered oppressive, backward or disrespectful of international law. At the same time, they were intent on preserving a rigorously apartheid social structure. The War of Independence (1946–49), was a particularly bloody and complex affair.

This 1933 stamp featuring rice cultivation fails to match the high standard of contemporary Dutch mainland issues.

NEVIS

**Scotland's lofty mountain peak
Gave its name to Nevis meek.**

Companion island to St Kitts with whom it is generally paired, Nevis has a separate postal administration. When it manages to avoid portraits of Princess Diana or Elvis Presley its stamps can be quite attractive, although hardly any celebrate the island's wonderful scenery (which is mostly Nevis Mountain). The island's name derives from Columbus's description of the clouds atop Nevis Peak as *Las Nieves,* or 'the snows', when he sighted the island. The OFFICIAL overprint means that this 1999 stamp was intended for government use (i.e., free for the user).

NEW CALEDONIA

**This longish island, far Down Under,
Is something of a natural wonder.**

This cigar-shaped island, a French 'unique collectivity' not far from Australia, is a major nickel producer. Although a rich region, wealth is unevenly divided between Europeans and the native Melanesian population. A referendum in 2018 narrowly voted against independence from France. As its name suggests, New Caledonia was once in British hands, and apparently reminded Captain Cook of the Highlands.

This attractive 1905 stamp features the Kagu, the island's flightless bird.

NEWFOUNDLAND

**This rugged place, not quite a nation,
Joined rather late the Federation.**

Last of the Canadian regions to join the Dominion of Canada (in 1949), Newfoundland conjures up images of rugged scenery, harsh winters and cod liver oil. Its stamps escaped (for the most part) the ponderous, duty-ridden issues of its bigger neighbour, the 1937 Coronation set being particularly attractive. This 1941 stamp features the missionary Sir William Grenfell, who took the welfare of the inhabitants of the Labrador Coast to heart: on his retirement the area boasted six hospitals, four hospital ships, seven nursing stations, two orphanages, two large schools, fourteen industrial centres, a cooperative lumber mill and a partridge in a pear tree.

NEW GUINEA

**Twenty-one shillings a guinea is worth:
The euro gives it a very wide berth.**

The second largest island in the world after Greenland, New Guinea is divided by a straight line down the middle, the western half now part of Indonesia, the eastern, Papua & New Guinea. Cook mapped the island group and named it the New Hebrides. According to Amnesty International, resistance to Indonesian rule has led to the death of more than 100,000 West Papuans as a result of government-sponsored violence.

This attractive 1939 airmail stamp, showing an aircraft over the Bulolo Goldfields, dates from Australia's tenure, shortly before Japan's invasion. Note Cook's galleon – and is that Man Friday?

NEW HEBRIDES

**All these islands, Scottish sounding,
Bathed by balmy seas astounding.**

Named after the Scottish archipelago, New Hebrides was ruled by France and Britain as a condominium from 1906 until its independence in 1980, when it became Vanuatu. The dual administration produced amazing duplication. There were two police forces with their own laws (including traffic laws), two health services, two education systems, two currencies and two prison systems. Separate British and French governments meant two immigration policies, two courts and two sets of corporation law. Inhabitants of the islands were given the choice of which government they wanted to be ruled by. Sounds like Belgium.

This attractive 1957 stamp gives an idea of the country's extremely mountainous terrain.

NEW SOUTH WALES

**A convict's home, but not for long;
A highly valued billabong.**

New South Wales was the first Australian colony to be established by the British. Now the most populated state in Australia, it was originally intended as a colony for felons, though some of the offenders may have done nothing worse than to protest injustice in Britain. Some of them indeed went on to achieve great things, for instance Thomas Watling, whose fine 1799 *View of Sydney* was the first painting of the city.

This stamp, issued in 1888 to celebrate the colony's centenary, features a kangaroo in the back garden.

NEW ZEALAND

**North Isle, South Isle, Middle Earth:
Sauron's homestead, little mirth.**

Early New Zealand issues, including this elegant 1935 Māori panel, can be very attractive; the first pictorials date from 1898.

Up until 2017 New Zealand issued Health Stamps, somewhat along the line of Switzerland's *Pro Juventute* stamps. The first appeared in 1931: they feature a smiling boy, and provoked sardonic comments in the Australian press (where else?), which described them as 'the world's worst stamps'. In fact, they are rather jolly.

NICARAGUA

**Lava, fauna, Lady Gaga:
These all rhyme with Nicaragua.**

Nicaraguan stamp design is a series of ups and downs. Its first stamp, issued in 1862, is a strikingly beautiful volcanic fantasy, promising great things. For the rest of the nineteenth century and, indeed, up until the late 1950s, Nicaraguan stamps are fairly turgid – as they are for most of Latin America (portraits of worthies, ponderous coats of arms). This 1962 orchid is from a better period; from the late 1960s things turn rather Cuban, which is to say Soviet-influenced. From the mid-1990s, in terms of design, the sun comes out, the clouds disappear, and Nicaragua can once more hold up its philatelic head with pride.

NIGER

**In all of Niger
Not one tiger.**

Named after the river which flows through its territory, French colonisation in Niger began in earnest in 1899, but owing to fierce resistance was consolidated only in 1922. Independence in 1960 ushered in periods of instability: coups, civil unrest, the introduction of sharia law and accusations of collusion in the slave trade. Education is free, but illiteracy rates are high, and health care is inadequate, especially in rural areas. And yet the country is rich in mineral resources, particularly uranium. Some of the mud-brick architecture, such as the Agadez Mosque (the tallest mud-brick structure in the world) is outstanding.

NIGER COAST PROTECTORATE

**Oil River, wider than a mile:
Crossing you was vile.**

The Niger Coast Protectorate was a British protectorate in the Oil Rivers area of present-day Nigeria, comprising the delta of the Niger River. Originally established as the Oil Rivers Protectorate in 1884, its status was confirmed at the Berlin Conference the same year. Britain, however, was unwilling to go to any expense to maintain it. Its name derived from the palm oil that was the chief product of the area.

The 1887 British set commemorating Queen Victoria's Jubilee is attractive in a jaunty *fin-de-siècle* sort of way.

NIGERIA

**Prosperous land, unending oil
Has put paid to years of toil.**

Given Nigeria's importance as an oil-producing nation (the tenth most important in the world, although little enough of its wealth is shared out in an equitable manner), it seemed apt to feature this somewhat stark 1973 stamp, one of a set of seventeen illustrating the country's economic activities. Nigerian stamp design is generally quite good, with many of the topics chosen relevant to the country itself (the same cannot be said of many of its neighbours).

NIUE

**Unpropitious land for rhyming;
Matter maybe just of timing.**

Niue, 'The Rock of Polynesia', is an internally self-governing island state in free association with New Zealand, and one of the Cook Islands, although administratively separate from them. Captain Cook named it Savage Island, no doubt following his cool reception there.

Great Britain issued stamps in honour of George VI's coronation for all of the British Commonwealth (that's a lot of stamp), but not all are similar. This design, with its incorporation of Māori wood carving, is one of the best, in my view. Even the overprint receives special treatment, something of a rarity. Later issues include more than their fair share of the Royals.

NORFOLK ISLAND

**Tiny island, lofty pines,
Convicts landed here betimes.**

This tiny island was administered by Australia until 1960, when local government was established. Some of the population are descendants of mutineers from *HMS Bounty,* who were transferred from the Pitcairns in 1856. Norfolk Island enjoyed a reputation as a harsh prison for convicts. Discovered by Captain Cook, who named it after the Duke of Norfolk, it was prized for its pine trees, used for building ships for the Royal Navy. Its main source of revenue today is tourism. Which is not surprising: it really is a most attractive place.

Norfolk Island's stamps are similar to Australia's; this one is a reminder of its grim past.

NORTH BORNEO

**Although the king was well intentioned,
North Borneo is best not mentioned.**

Now the Malaysian state of Sabah (q.v.), formerly under the administration of the North Borneo Company before becoming a crown colony in 1946. After WWII the North Borneo Company handed over the territory to the Colonial Office in return for a hefty cash payment.

Many of North Borneo's stamps are very beautiful, particularly the pictorial sets of 1894 and 1897. This striking 1939 stamp is democratically inscribed in English, Arabic and Malay.

NORTH GERMAN CONFEDERATION

**Itsy-bitsy little states:
Bismarck's Germany awaits.**

Much of Northern Germany was included in this short-lived postal administration, which saw the light of day in 1868 prior to joining the post-unification Reichspost in 1871. Two currencies were used: Groschen and Thaler for the Northern District, Kreuzer and Gulden for the Southern District. No prizes for this stamp design, although the delicate frame made up of what looks like post horns and winged railway wheels (a symbol we see in early Belgian railway stamps) may have faded with time (yellow being a dodgy colour in printing).

NORTH KOREA

**Pacific cod, respects no borders,
Swims around ignoring orders.**

North Korean stamps are every bit as ugly as the regime that produces them, and quite a few are replete with navel-gazing slogans ('Children grow up happily in the bosom of Father Marshal Kim Il Sung', for the International Year of the Child, 1979). The early issues, dating from 1950, are crude, doubtless as a result of the economic deprivation felt in a country at war, but many of the 1960s issues are quite pleasing, being less slick than later ones, and modestly designed to boot. This Pacific cod looks pleasantly surprised to feature on a stamp.

NORTHERN NIGERIA

**Northern Nigeria, Southern Nigeria:
None of these places is far from Liberia.**

Northern Nigeria, a British protectorate established in 1900, lasted until 1914, when it was incorporated into Nigeria proper. Its short history was bloody, although following a brutally repressed Mahdist revolt in 1906 the use of military force was replaced by an emphasis on taxation and administration. The north-south divide apparently persists in Nigeria to this day: borders drawn for the benefit of colonial administrations often rode roughshod over ethnic grouping.

I find this 1912 stamp simple and elegant; a crown hovers over the monarch, while ornate theatrical curtains have just been drawn aside, as if to say, 'The colonial show must go on, chaps.'

NORTHERN RHODESIA

**To honour Rhodes they named this place,
A haven of divided race.**

Formerly the British South Africa Company (BSAC), now present-day Zambia. Northern Rhodesia's main resource was copper, which made the BSAC very rich; little of the wealth went to the miners. The BSAC owned the mines and creamed off the royalties, and the British government taxed the rest. British dependence on undisturbed copper production in WWII meant that white mine workers were allowed to maintain a colour bar, one of a handful of British colonies to practise it (the others being Southern Rhodesia, Kenya, South Africa and South West Africa).

Here, George V presides over a savannah fantasy.

NORWAY

**Hedda Gabler, trolls and fjords,
Packs of reindeer live like lords.**

Ceded to Sweden by Denmark in 1814, Norway became independent in 1905. Norwegian stamps are understated, particularly the monochrome issues up until the 1960s. Bright colours begin to predominate from the 1980s, but without sacrificing good taste.

This beautiful 1938 scene of Jølster in the Sunnfjord was part of a tourist propaganda set. Note the elegant 'surround' for the numerals and the crisp postmark dated 22 April 1939, less than one year before the German invasion.

NYSALAND PROTECTORATE

**Protectorates they called these places,
Electorates that had white faces.**

'In 1891 the British established the Nyasaland Districts Protectorate, which was called ... Nyasaland from 1907. Under the colonial regime, roads and railways were built, and the cultivation of cash crops by European settlers was introduced. On the other hand, the colonial administration did little to enhance the welfare of the African majority, because of commitment to the interests of European settlers ... Furthermore, between 1951 and 1953 the colonial government decided to join the colonies of Southern and Northern Rhodesia and Nyasaland in the Federation of Rhodesia and Nyasaland, against bitter opposition from their African inhabitants.' *(Encyclopaedia Britannica)*. On independence, Nyasaland became Malaŵi, which means 'lake' in Swahili.

OLDENBURG

**Its days they were numbered
When Bismarck he thundered.**

A former Grand Duchy in North Germany, which joined the North German Federation (q.v.) in 1867.

Germany before unification was a patchwork quilt of states and statelets. Oldenburg, for instance, consisted of three widely separated territories: Oldenburg itself, close to the Dutch border; Eutin in Schleswig-Holstein; and Birkenfeld in the Rhine Palatinate.

Some effort has gone into the design of this imperforate 1859 stamp, but the overall effect is amateurish.

OMAN

**Roamin' in the gloamin' on the bonnie banks o' Clyde,
Roamin' in the Oman wi' ma lassie by ma side.**

Formerly the Sultanate of Muscat & Oman (q.v.), renamed Oman in 1971. This view of Matrah (Muttrah), painted in 1809 and incorporated into this 1972 design, is a delight. Sadly, later issues are mostly horrid gaudy affairs, proof if it were needed that money does not guarantee good design.

ORANGE FREE STATE

Free Orange State, now that sounds better:
More the spirit than the letter.

The name Orange Free State is derived from the Orange River, which in turn was named in honour of the Dutch ruling family, the House of Orange. To an Irishman, the term is comical: virulent Ulster Unionists refer derisively to citizens of the Republic of Ireland as 'Free Staters'. The Orange Free State was a British possession from 1848 to 1854, independent as a Boer republic from 1854 to 1899 and annexed by Britain in 1900, before joining the Union of South Africa in 1910. King, springbok and gnu adorn this cheerful 1903 issue, inscribed ORANGE RIVER COLONY.

PAHANG

**Orangutang, spelt with a 'g',
Rhymes with Pahang – would you agree?**

Pahang became one of the Federated Malay States in 1895 and joined the Federation of Malaya in 1963. Pahang consists mostly of dense forest, with river transport of great importance in the interior owing to few roads, an environment wonderfully described in Conrad's *Almayer's Folly*.

This 1950 stamp features Sultan Sir Abu Bakar, popular with his subjects but not with other Malay rulers, owing to his penchant for marrying commoners. The rendition of the Government Offices is mediocre.

PAKISTAN

**The British left, down to a man,
Giving rise to Pakistan.**

Pakistan's first stamps were King George VI Indian stamps overprinted PAKISTAN, issued in 1947. Muhammed Ali Jinnah, the country's founder (much admired by Churchill), features quite frequently; later stamps cover a wide variety of topics and are well designed and colourful. The finest set, in my opinion, is that of 1961, which features monochrome views of the Khyber Pass, the Shalimar Gardens in Lahore and the Chota Sona Masjid Gateway in East Pakistan (now Bangladesh). This lovely stamp shows a view of mountains at Gilgit, and is overprinted SERVICE, indicating administrative use. Old habits die hard: official and service stamps were part and parcel of the Raj, and the last Pakistani service stamps were issued as late as 1990.

PALESTINE

**A stitch in time
Might have saved Palestine.**

'In Palestine we do not propose even to go through the form of consulting the wishes of the present inhabitants of the country' (Anglo-French Declaration of 1918).

Palestine issued its own stamps from 1918, following the collapse of the Ottoman Empire, and ceased issuing with the establishment of the State of Israel in 1948. Following the Oslo accord, The Palestinian Authority began issuing stamps in 1994 for use in the Gaza Strip and ever-dwindling West Bank. This 1927 issue features the Citadel in Jerusalem, and is inscribed in Hebrew, English and Arabic.

PANAMA

**Flag of convenience, narrow canal,
Panama's certainly far from banal.**

In 1501 Vasco Núñez de Balboa was the first European to explore the Atlantic coast of the Isthmus of Panama. As head of the colony, Balboa, by the use of persuasion and force (a favourite tactic was letting his hounds tear recalcitrant Indians to pieces) subjugated most of the native population. In September 1513 he reached the Pacific Ocean and claimed Panama for his king.

Construction of the Panama Canal began in 1880 but was beset by disease and financial chicanery. The US exploited this situation by buying out the rights for the completion of the canal, which opened in 1914, at the same time assisting Panamanian revolutionaries in their quest for independence from Colombia.

PAPUA

**Papua's quite hot and sticky;
Hiking trips are rather tricky.**

Before becoming Papua New Guinea (q.v.), Papua was – well, Papua. The first issues were inscribed BRITISH NEW GUINEA; from 1907, stamps such as this very attractive *lakatoi* (native canoe) were inscribed PAPUA. After Japan's defeat Australian stamps were used, before the introduction of the combined issues of Papua New Guinea in 1952.

PAPUA NEW GUINEA

**In 1973
Papua ceased to be.**

Papua New Guinea forms the eastern half of the second biggest island in the world. Formerly under Australian administration, it gained independence in 1975. Separated from Australia by the Torres Strait a mere 8,000 years ago, Papua New Guinea is extremely mountainous; the northern limestone region is a harsh area of endless ridges of jagged rock covered in impenetrable rainforest. Stamp design, largely Australian, is attractive, as can be seen in the first set issued in 1952, which features this bird of paradise.

PARAGUAY

**Ah! To do or die
In Paraguay!**

This landlocked country has had its fair share of turbulence. Not many wars have been fought on South American soil in recent history, but the Chaco War between Paraguay and Bolivia (1932–35), fought over oil reserves, ended in defeat for the former. (In the Triple Alliance War of 1846 to 1848 Paraguay had already lost territory to Argentina and Brazil.)

A unique linguistic phenomenon is to be found in Paraguay: more people speak the Guarani language than Spanish. RUTA DE GRANDEZA HACIA EL PORVENIR: 'Path of greatness to the future', so this pleasing 1939 stamp tells us, issued to mark peace between Paraguay and Bolivia.

PATIALA

**Punjabi state in the Convention,
Queen Victoria's invention.**

Yet another of those convention states in the Punjab. The Darshani Gate (the main gate of the Qila Mubarak) is well worth a visit. Patiala is also famous for a style of turban, the Patiala Shahi Pagg.

High values quite often get VIP treatment in stamp design: here Edward VII's Raj surrenders itself to Art Nouveau brio.

PENANG

**Pula Pinang's lovely stamps,
Philatelically champs.**

Penang is a Malaysian island state. Owing to its location in the Strait of Malacca it was considered of strategic interest to the British, and in 1826 Penang merged with Malacca, Singapore and Labuan to form the Straits Settlements (q.v.).

Although the Malay States are all now part of Malaysia, they continue to issue their own stamps. These are mostly identical in design, and feature regional flora and fauna, such as this cheerful hibiscus job issued in 1979. The higher values are Malaysian national issues.

PERAK

**It seems we've seen this stamp before!
(Writing rhymes is such a chore.)**

Perak, another of the Malayan states, is rich in tin reserves, which has made it the constant subject of local and international incursions. By all accounts the Perak Tong Cave Temple is staggeringly beautiful, while the railway station in Ipoh, a splendid colonial pile, is known locally as the Taj Mahal of Ipoh.

This stamp looks identical to the previous one, but in fact the coat of arms is different, and is surmounted by a sultan chappie.

PERU

Human sacrifice is bad.
Machu Picchu's closed. I'm glad.

In 1870, to mark the twentieth anniversary of the country's first railway, Peru issued one of the world's first commemorative stamps. Nicknamed the *trencito*, or 'little train', it was produced on a French-made device (the so-called 'Lecoq' press) that was used to print, emboss and cut imperforate stamps from paper strips.

Peruvian stamps follow the South American pattern: dull to begin with, gradual improvement from the 1950s on, markedly so from 2000. This 1936 stamp catches the eye: it shows an Inca postal runner (EL CHASQUI CORREOS DE LOS INCAS) with the Andes in the background, surrounded by a delightful, Inca-inspired frame.

PHILIPPINES

**Long ago the Spanish came,
Gave these islands the king's name.**

Ceded by Spain to the US after the brutal war of 1898, the Philippines gained independence in 1946. An archipelago consisting of 1,700 islands, the country takes its name from Philip II of Spain. The Philippines was under Spanish rule for 333 years and US administration for forty-eight. English is an official language, and the Philippines is predominantly Roman Catholic, rare for an Asian country.

This 1880 stamp is anything but beautiful: standard issue Spanish King Alfonso XII (a popular and wise ruler). Later issues are almost uniformly dull, and oddly similar to many South American issues.

PITCAIRN ISLANDS

**Fletcher had a row with Bligh,
Left the *Bounty*, waved goodbye.***

Pitcairn Island is the only inhabited island of a group of four. The story of Fletcher and Bligh is well known; less well known is the fact that some islanders emigrated to Norfolk Island (q.v.) in 1856, or that the dialect, Pitkern, is a mixture of Tahitian and eighteenth-century English (Ye like-a sum whettles? = Would you like some food?)

The first stamps date from 1940; here, the king's portrait depicts him as a sad, distant figure, and the frame is far from harmonious. The tiny population of just fifty people produces stamps far beyond its own postal needs, for a predominantly British overseas market; this may explain the number of issues devoted to British royalty.

In fact, it was the other way round.

POLAND

**Gdansk and Cracow, Warsaw too,
Just the land for me and you.**

Considering that Poland as a nation disappeared between 1782 and 1918, parcelled out between Russia, Prussia and Austria in the 'Partitions of Poland', its re-emergence as a modern nation state was nothing short of miraculous. This was in large part due to the efforts of the Polish diaspora and nineteenth-century artists such as Chopin and Mickiewicz, and later the pianist Ignacy Paderewski, who influenced the thinking of Woodrow Wilson on the subject of Polish independence.

This stamp was issued to mark the creation of Poland's first modern constitution.

PORTUGAL

**In this medieval knight
Do all philatelists delight.**

As a child I had a soft spot for this stamp, and, along with others (including The British 'Children's Toys' set of 1963 and the Bulgarian 'Ancient Trees' set of 1967), it helped trigger a newfound interest in stamp collecting later in life. I expect that many collectors have had the same experience.

Portugal's early issues are awfully dull (*vid.* the dreaded 'Ceres' set of 1912, with eighty-five identical values), but today's issues are among the world's most attractive.

PORTUGUESE GUINEA

**Lusitanian colonials
Scribbled testimonials.**

Following independence Portuguese Guinea was renamed Guinea-Bissau after its capital, Bissau, in order to distinguish it from its neighbour Guinea (q.v.). A murderous campaign of 'pacification' in Portuguese Guinea took place from 1913 to 1915, provoking a widespread outcry. Calls for independence in the late 1950s were savagely repressed by Lisbon until the coup of 1974, when the new democratic Portuguese government acceded to the request. This 1969 stamp features the coat of arms* of King Manuel I of Portugal.

**'Of all coats the most useless' (Gibbon)*

PORTUGUESE INDIA

**Garcia Orta, medical man,
Lived here, got a lovely tan.**

At one time several tracts of land in India were in the hands of the Portuguese, the most important being Goa. 'He who has seen Goa need not see Lisbon', according to a Portuguese expression, and Goa's architectural heritage is both splendid and quite different from that of the rest of the sub-continent. The Portuguese eventually relinquished Goa with very ill grace in 1961, no doubt unwilling to take on the might of the Indian army.

Garcia Orta was a pioneer of tropical medicine.

PORTUGUESE TIMOR

Timor et tremor,
Motet for a tenor.

The *Encyclopaedia Britannica* succinctly explains the roots of the conflict in East Timor: 'The Portuguese began trading with Timor, probably for sandalwood, about 1520. In 1613 the Dutch established themselves in Kupang, in a sheltered bay at the south-western tip of the island, and the Portuguese moved to the north and east. Treaties effective in 1860 and 1914 between Portugal and the Netherlands divided the island and set the boundaries that existed until 1975, when Indonesian troops invaded and occupied East Timor.'

PRUSSIA

**Take off the 'P', it's merely Russia –
Which might just lead to repercussia.**

Prussia at one time comprised large swathes not only of Germany, but also modern-day Poland and Kaliningrad. The Teutonic Knights, Frederic the Great (the longest reigning member of the Hohenzollern family), the brothers von Humboldt, Blücher's timely arrival at Waterloo – the list of Prussian notables goes on and on. Prussia's brief stamp-issuing life – from 1850 to 1867, at which point it joined the North German Confederation (q.v.) – is undistinguished in terms of design.

PUERTO RICO

**Status as United State
Has been much discussed of late.**

What did King Alfonso XII of Spain make, one wonders, of distant Puerto Rico? Today the island is self-governing in association with the US, to whom it was ceded by Spain in 1898. Quite apart from the question of whether or not Puerto Rico desires to become the 51st State, the US cavils at the idea of absorbing an entirely Hispanic island, and one which (initially at least) would make significant demands on the treasury. However, when Governor Alejandro García Padilla announced in 2015 that Puerto Rico could no longer meet its debt obligations, the island was treated like a state (and not a municipality) under the US federal bankruptcy code and therefore could *not* declare itself bankrupt. A case of *el gringo* having his cake and eating it.

QATAR

**This pretty stamp with overprint
Doth boast a faintly lilac tint.**

Historically Qatar has had very humble beginnings: from nomad to pearl fisher, from pirate to oil sheikh. It declared independence in 1971. Qatar's being awarded the 2022 World Cup brought new scrutiny to the country's domestic affairs, particularly its reliance on the *kafalah* labour system (according to Qatar, since abolished), in which low-paid foreign workers endured appalling conditions.

The stamp featured is one of the celebrated 'Wilding' set of British definitives issued on the Queen's accession to the throne. They are masterpieces of understated elegance, and justifiably popular with collectors.

QUEENSLAND

**Named after a queen
Who's never been.**

Stamps for the individual Australian States prior to federation are mostly turgid affairs, so this elegant 1860 issue featuring a youthful Queen Victoria surrounded by delicate filigree comes as a welcome surprise. Well, not so youthful in 1860, but never mind. The engraving was by William Humphrys, based on the painting by Alfred Edward Chalon, commissioned on the occasion of Victoria's first address to the House of Lords.

RÉUNION

**Sounds like a pupils' get-together,
But once you're there you'll like the weather.**

My first real taste of tropical sun was during a concert trip to Réunion, where I got so badly sunburnt that I had to lie in a bath of tepid water for three days.

This attractive 1907 stamp (I have always loved the combination of red and green) features a handy map. The 1933 definitive series is one of the most attractive of the French colonial issues, but sadly there are only three designs for a total of forty-one stamps in the set. From 1949 to 1975 Réunion used French stamps surcharged CFA, the local currency, after which it used – and still uses – unsurcharged French stamps, since it is now a French *département*.

RHODESIA

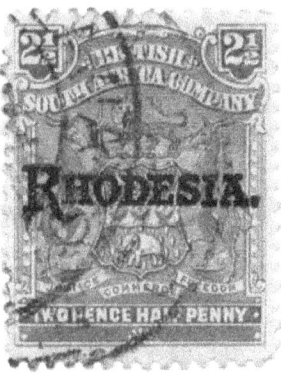

**Named after an unpleasant man
Who a colonial rush began.**

Just as with the Mozambique Company (q.v.), the practice of granting a charter to private companies was not unknown to British colonial expansion. A colony implied a minimum engagement to invest in the infrastructure of the area colonised, in terms of transport, health, education etc. But the British South Africa Company, featured on this 1909 stamp overprinted RHODESIA, served to expropriate lands and people purely for profit and at no expense to the taxpayer. Cecil Rhodes and his cronies were itinerant thugs, all too happy to carry the white man's burden. Note the mendacious inscription at the base of this appropriately hideous stamp.

RHODESIA & NYASALAND

**2/6d black & red,
In the middle the Queen's head.**

The Federation of Rhodesia and Nyasaland, also called The Central African Federation, a political unit created in 1953 and lasting until 1963, embraced the British settler-dominated colony of Southern Rhodesia (Zimbabwe), the territories of Northern Rhodesia (Zambia) and Nyasaland (Malaŵi), all under the control of the British Colonial Office.

Britain was persuaded to support federation by economic arguments and in the hope of creating a multiracial state based on partnership, in order to counter South Africa's racial policies. Blacks in Northern Rhodesia and Nyasaland, however, consistently opposed federation, which they feared would be dominated by Southern Rhodesia.

RIO MUNI

**This depiction's quite mendacious,
Not to say a little tasteless.**

Spain's colonial ventures in Africa were limited to enclaves and small slivers of land; perhaps, having had its fingers badly burnt in South America, it was less than keen to repeat the experience in Africa. Rio Muni, together with Fernando Póo (q.v.), became Equatorial Guinea.

Prior to its first issues (of which this stamp is one) it used the stamps of Spanish Guinea (q.v.). Nowadays the stereotypes seen on this stamp ('Native boy reading book', complete with hovering-in-the-background priest) strike a jarring note.

ROMANIA

**The Danube has her estuary here,
Ukraine, Moldova are quite near.**

Dullish portraits of princes and kings adorn Romania's stamps up until 1903, when rather attractive pictorial issues first appear. Stamps of the communist period are propaganda-rich and generally fairly awful, although this 1957 one, from a set of the fauna of the Danube Delta, never fails to charm. Post-Ceaușescu there is also little to write home about: one has to wait until the mid-2000s to hear an individual voice in Romanian stamp design. The first Romanian issues were for Moldavia, (not to be confused with Moldova, q.v.) and, after 1861, for Wallachia also; the two regions then fused to become Romania. Such stamps are highly sought-after.

RUANDA-URUNDI

©Bpost

**Luckless native climbing tree,
Making white men rich – no fee.**

Two swathes of territory were granted to Belgium as war reparation in 1919: a small area in western Germany which became the East Cantons of Belgium, and part of the German colony of Tanganyika, which became Ruanda-Urundi. On independence Ruanda-Urundi became two separate countries, Rwanda and Burundi. Tragically, the ethnic divide between Hutu and Tutsi, which had been deliberately fostered by the German administration, persisted under Belgian rule, which lasted until 1962.

RUSSIA

**Five-Year plans in tones uplifting:
Lots of grain here, ripe for sifting.**

Russian stamp design can be categorised as follows: the early tsarist issues, elegant if a little dull; the crude issues of the early Bolshevik years; a marked improvement from the 1930s, with the best issues dating from the 1950s, and, finally, anything post-Sputnik, featuring a gradual decline into over-production and garish colours, which has continued (with some exceptions) until the present day.

I love the muted colours of this 1956 'Harvesting' stamp, typical of issues of the 1950s. One of a set of seven stamps on an agricultural theme.

RWANDA

**Arbitrary borders, total mayhem.
'Take up our arms and let us slay them.'**

Sometimes a stamp catalogue tells you all you need to know: Stanley Gibbons, in its 2016 world edition, lists no issues for Rwanda between 1993 and 1998; presumably stamp production was low on the list of priorities during that dreadful period. On a more positive note, the *Encyclopaedia Britannica* tells us that 'The landscape is reminiscent of a tropical Switzerland.'

This attractive, well-designed stamp is one of a set of four issued in 1992 to mark the International Nutrition Conference in Rome; calm before the storm.

SAARLAND

**O'er Saarland long they bickered,
For the flames of pride still flickered.**

Following WWI Saarland's coal mines were awarded to France, and Saarland was placed under the administration of the League of Nations for fifteen years, at the end of which time a plebiscite permitted the inhabitants to choose between being part of France or Germany. In that plebiscite, held in 1935, more than ninety per cent of the inhabitants of Saar voted for its return to Germany. Following WWII, France once again occupied Saarland, but in 1956 it was agreed to return it once more to Germany.

SABAH

**Someone said, 'Let's change its name,
For North Borneo's far too plain.'**

Formerly North Borneo, Sabah is now part of Malaysia. Much of its eastern portion is claimed by the Philippines. The handy map shown on this North Borneo issue overprinted SABAH tells you exactly where you are. In 1877 a private syndicate (chartered in 1881 as the British North Borneo Company) obtained land grants from the sultans of Brunei and Sulu, and took pains to invest in infrastructure. The Japanese occupation destroyed the economy of the region. Sabah joined the Federation of Malaya in 1963; in common with the other states in Malaysia, it issues its own stamps (invariably flora and fauna), except for the high values, which are national.

ST CHRISTOPHER

**This friendly saint has lost his job –
Did he have dealings with the mob?**

St Christopher is the larger of the two islands that go to make up St Kitts & Nevis. It boasts the aptly named Mount Liamuiga (Mount Misery), a volcano 3,800 feet high, which, as its name suggests, is notoriously difficult to climb.

The island first issued stamps in 1870, including this fairly standard Queen Vic, but these were superseded in 1890 by general issues for the Leeward Islands (q.v.).

ST HELENA

**To this island so remote
Came Napoleon in a boat.**

Apart from modest issues in 2001 and 2008 marking the 180th anniversary of Napoleon's death and the 150th anniversary of the purchase of Longwood House respectively, there is no sense of philatelic jubilation at the fact that this remote island is world-renowned for having been Napoleon's second prison. The issues from Edward VII to early Queen Elizabeth II are well worth collecting; this attractive three-master (was it the ship that transported Napoleon from France?) is the badge of the colony. Later issues fall into the trap of modern British Commonwealth stamps, particularly those of island nations: a mite too much royalty for my taste.

ST KITTS & NEVIS

**Ageing king in festive colour:
Without these isles, life would be duller.**

ST CHRISTOPHER NEVIS ANGUILLA, so runs the inscription on this late George VI stamp issued in 1952. In fact, Anguilla later broke away from the partnership, on account of interinsular tensions. The islands are part of the Leeward Islands group, and used issues for the Leewards concurrently with their own until 1956. From 1980 St Kitts & Nevis had their own separate postal administrations.

This stamp is pleasant enough but lacks the imaginative flair of earlier George VI colonial issues, notably those issued in 1938. The pedestrian pennants are a far cry from the references to native art we find in the Fijian stamp (q.v.), for example.

ST LUCIA

The Pitons, **what a jolly spot:
To live near here I'd pay a lot.**

Almost all British colonial issues from the year 1938 (the year following George VI's coronation) are attractive, and this gorgeous scene featuring *The Pitons* is a good introduction to the dramatic scenery of this small Caribbean island, one of the Windwards. St Lucia see-sawed between Britain and France, so much so that along with Dominica its population is mostly Roman Catholic, and a French patois is still spoken. At the time of emancipation in 1834, the island counted 13,000 slaves.

ST VINCENT

Bathing beach at Villa:
Don't forget your pilla.

The British acquired St Vincent in 1763 as part of the settlement of the Treaty of Paris that followed the Seven Years War. The native Caribs resisted occupation throughout the late 1700s, but they were eventually exiled to an island off the coast of Honduras following their surrender in 1796. Their descendants, known as Garifuna, are to be found in Belize, Guatemala, Honduras and Nicaragua; there are also large numbers of Garifuna in California and New York. Nowadays the island is a tax haven, and, judging by photos I have seen, overflowing with vulgar villas. It was all so different at the time of this stamp's issue in 1938, stern in aspect but with an attractive coil-patterned frame. Later issues fall into the royalty/butterfly trap.

SAMOA

**When stocks run low you must bisect,
For if you don't you'll lose respect.**

In 1962 Western Samoa, following periods under German and New Zealand rule, became the first Pacific nation of its size to gain independence.

This 1886 stamp is bisected, presumably meaning that stocks had run low (Samoa being remote), or that postal rates had changed. Bisects are comparatively rare, since they were no longer needed once new stocks arrived. Understandably, such stamps are worthless if not 'on cover', i.e., on an envelope. Were eyebrows raised at the local post office when the scissors were brandished, I wonder? Later Samoan issues are typical of small islands trying to make a few bob out of stamps: fairly awful.

SAN MARINO

**Rising high above the plains,
San Marino has no trains.**

The Republic of San Marino can trace its origin to the early fourth century when, according to tradition, a group of Christians led by St Marinus settled there to escape persecution. Its independence was respected by Napoleon and later by Garibaldi: presumably its impregnable location would have stopped any military commander in his tracks.

San Marino was the first country in the world to abolish the death penalty. One of its main sources of revenue is stamps, markedly Italian in design. This beautiful 1944 issue features Mount Titano, on which San Marino is built.

SANTANDER

**Santandrines are from Santander;
Alexandrines, Alexander.**

Was ever duller stamp issued? Santander was one of the *departamentos* of the Granadine Confederation, which later became Colombia. It issued stamps between 1884 and 1903.

Coats of arms were very popular with the newly-liberated-shortly-to-be-coalesced-into-one-country stamps of South America. They smack of stuffed shirt, as if the nascent South America was unwilling to throw off the dusty accoutrements of Mother Spain.

SAO TOMÉ E PRINCIPE

**Graced by Lisbon's kindly rule,
Behold Sao Tomé now, a jewel.**

The two small islands making up this nation state were formerly Portuguese possessions, originally used as an *entrepôt* for slaves en route to Brazil. Slavery was abolished in 1875, but contract workers brought in from Angola, Cape Verde and Mozambique suffered conditions akin to slavery until 1910, to such a degree that Cadbury's boycotted the islands' cacao production in 1909. Corruption and absentee landlords contributed to civil unrest, culminating in the Batépa Massacre of 1953, which Portugal claimed was necessary in order to put down a communist plot (in fact, no such plot ever existed).

This cheerful stamp, one of a 1952 set honouring Portuguese explorers, was issued shortly before the massacre.

SARAWAK

**The last White Rajah of Sarawak
Gave up his throne – alas, alack!**

Sarawak, the biggest of the Malayan states, comprises the north-western part of the island of Borneo. James Brooke, an English adventurer and a former military officer of the East India Com-pany, visited the territory in 1839 and aided the sultan in sup-pressing a revolt. As a reward for his services, Brooke was installed as Rajah of Sarawak in 1841, effectively founding a dynasty of 'White Rajahs'. The White Rajahs did their best to prevent the indigenous peoples of Sarawak from being exploited by West-ern business interests. Bankrupted by the Japanese occupation, Britain took over the administration of the territory from 1946 to 1963, at which point Sarawak joined the Malayan Federation.

SAUDI ARABIA

**The grimmest stamp I've ever seen;
To this hot land I've never been.**

Saudi Arabian postal history reflects the turmoil that surrounded the creation of the state. Taking advantage of Turkish involvement in WWI, the Hejaz, a region in the north-west of the country, broke away from Ottoman rule in 1916, but was overrun by the Sultan of Nejd in 1925. Stamps for the Hejaz were issued from 1916, and for the Hejaz and Nejd from 1926. In 1932 the two regions merged to become Saudi Arabia.

Saudi issues until the late 1960s are sober and well-designed, after which oil revenue spells a downturn in quality, with the exception of some remarkably attractive flora and fauna issues in the 1990s. This 1976 stamp is not actually that awful, but the postmark is hideous. An oil stain?

SAXONY

**King Johann I, a handsome fellow,
Attired (I think) in black and yellow.**

Saxony has changed enormously in size and importance throughout the ages: at one point it ruled Bohemia, but its enthusiastic alliance with Napoleon was dearly paid for at the Congress of Vienna in terms of lost territory. King Frederick Augustus II was deposed by a revolutionary uprising in 1848 but was restored to power by Prussian troops a week later. His son Johann I, who features on this foliage-rich 1855 stamp, did much to promote freedom of trade and the development of the railway system, as well as translating Dante's *Divine Comedy* into German. In 1868 Saxony joined the North German Confederation, whose stamps it then used.

SELANGOR

**This portly man and his pet tiger
Ruled Selangor from a hang-glider.**

One of the Malaysian states, Selangor relinquished its state capital Kuala Lumpur to the federal government in 1974. Kuala Lumpur boasts an enormous Guinness Brewery (apparently the Dublin brew is thought to be an aphrodisiac), which opened in 1893, servicing thirsty non-Muslims ever since.

This attractive 1960 stamp features Sultan Salahuddin Abdul Aziz (1926—2001) and his pet tiger.

SENEGAL

**Awfully bally far,
That rally in Dakar.**

When Governor Louis Léon César Faidherbe of Senegal retired in 1865, the French controlled most of the territory of modern Senegal, where the cultivation and export of peanuts yielded great economic benefits for the colonists. Senegal at the time of this stamp's issue was part of *Afrique Occidentale Française,* or French West Africa, a vast area comprising eight French colonial territories: Mauritania, Senegal, French Sudan, French Guinea, Ivory Coast, Upper Volta, Dahomey and Niger.

This market scene is attractive enough, although rather poorly executed. Presumably there were budgetary restrictions at the time of its issue, since the stamp is one of a set of forty-three using the same design, but with the colours changed.

SERBIA

**The Serbs fought bravely in the war,
When Panzers into Belgrade tore.**

To understand recent Serbian history, it is necessary to return to the year 1867, which saw the establishment of the Austro-Hungarian 'Dual Monarchy'. Croats were exposed to a regime of 'magyarisation', while at the same time the abolition of the old Military Frontier meant that Serbs became part of an expanded Croatia. Hungary played off Serb and Croat for its own political aims, provoking Serbo-Croat hostility for the first time.

The first strictly constitutional monarch of his country, King Petar I features on this formal, somewhat fussy issue dating from 1905.

SEYCHELLES

**Shey shells seychelles
On the sheyshore.**

Seychelles' stamps, curiously enough, did not follow the line-engraved issues of 1938 used for most of the British colonies; instead, a not unattractive lithograph design appeared in 1938 and 1952 for George VI, and in 1954 for the Queen, featuring tortoises, pirogues, maps and palm trees, as well as this fabulous-looking creature, the sailfish. Reputed to be the fastest fish alive (speeds of up to sixty-eight mph have been recorded), it has a dorsal fin running the full length of its body. A gruesome video on YouTube shows just how difficult it is to fillet – which bodes well for its survival.

SICILY

**King 'Bomba' had a short-lived reign:
G. Garibaldi was to blame.**

During the nineteenth century Sicily was a major centre of revolutionary movements: in 1860, as a result of Giuseppe Garibaldi's revolt, it was liberated from the Bourbons, and in the following year was incorporated into the United Kingdom of Italy. I thought initially that this 1859 stamp featuring King 'Bomba' was a joke, but King Ferdinand II of Naples and Sicily (1810—1859) was nicknamed just that owing to his bombardment of Messina in 1848. His son, nicknamed 'Bombalino' (how else?) ruled for a few months before being overthrown by Garibaldi. For all his faults, 'Bomba' inaugurated the first Italian railway. Stamp design was not one of his talents.

SIERRA LEONE

**This feisty lady, carrying rice,
Is hoping for a decent price.**

The name Sierra Leone derives from the Portuguese *Serra Leoa* or 'Lion Mountains'. The British appreciated the importance of the world's largest natural harbour situated in present-day Freetown, the country's capital. A tax on huts (of anything up to half a year's salary) was imposed in 1898, provoking major unrest.

Sierra Leone, along with Tonga, hit on the novel idea of issuing stamps in unorthodox shapes such as a map of Africa, an eagle, a diamond etc., but more recent issues, while well designed, show the same lack of interest in native culture that we see replicated in other African countries: Mona Lisa, Pope John Paul II, Lady Di, Elvis and company grace the country's philatelic canon.

SINGAPORE

**The Queen looks down on Raffles's pile,
But only for a little while.**

Originally claimed for Britain by Sir Stamford Raffles of the East India Company (to the great chagrin of the Dutch), Singapore is now the biggest port in South East Asia. Tin and rubber were originally the source of the city-state's wealth. Britain opposed Singapore's joining the Malaysian Federation in 1963 on the grounds that its majority Chinese population might cause problems relating to ethnic conflict in future times, which no doubt influenced the Malaysian government's polite request to Singapore to leave the Federation in 1965.

The Raffles Hotel (if I'm not mistaken, visible on the stamp) is a remarkably elegant pile. Rooms are expensive: at €540 a night definitely not for the riffle-raffle.

SLOVAKIA

©art from the *Big Pets* by Lane Smith, 1991

**If you admire good graphic art,
Slovakia's the place to start.**

Czechoslovak stamp design was a beacon of artistic excellence in the communist era – compare its issues to those of the DDR, Poland or Hungary – and Slovakia certainly seems to be continuing the tradition. Pre-communist issues (i.e., from 1939 to 1948) are fairly dull, but the first post-communist issues include a stunning definitive set on the theme of Slovak architecture. The penchant for imaginative graphic art is nowhere better illustrated than this 1993 issue, marking the Fourteenth Biennial Exhibition of Book Illustrations for Children, Bratislava (although the illustration is actually by the American artist Lane Smith).

SLOVENIA

**O, Triglav proud! O, mountain high!
On your steep slopes so many die!**

Slovenia's first stamps are Yugoslav issues overprinted in Italian or German during the war years, such as the 1945 issue bearing the inscription PROVINZ LAIBACH (Hitler considering Slovenia to be part of the Reich).

Of all the ex-Iron Curtain countries, Slovenia produces the most exuberant stamps, hardly less beautiful than its scenery. This stamp, dated 2001 (I think – I cannot find it in my catalogue), shows a mountain hut skilfully placed on a background of contour lines, a lovely example of the sort of thing for which stamp design is particularly well suited.

SOLOMON ISLANDS

**Cheerful hues, engraver's skill:
For this fine stamp I've paid a mill.**

The Solomon Islands were so named because of a belief that they were the source of the gold used in the building of King Solomon's Temple. The British Solomon Islands were declared a protectorate in 1893, mainly to forestall a threat of annexation by France. Islanders were punished harshly for perceived offences against colonial law and order.

Predictably, the most interesting stamps are the pictorial issues of 1939 and 1956, which are truly stunning: the summit of colonial stamp design.

SOMALIA

**These dirty postmarks make it plain:
Don't try to use this stamp again!**

Pre-civil war Somali stamps are remarkably attractive, although the one I have chosen, good as far as football stamps go, is no beauty (the postmarks are admittedly something of a joke). Somalia's first stamps date from the time of the Italian occupation, and are just as attractive as those of another Italian colony, Libya. Worryingly, Stanley Gibbons lists no issues after 1991 – a sure sign of civic meltdown.

SOMALILAND PROTECTORATE

**This regal couple, hand in hand,
Protected all Somaliland.**

The British Somaliland Protectorate Administration was established in the 1880s as a reaction to territorial ambitions on the part of France, Egypt and Italy, with an eye to protecting all-important Aden.

The first issues for the protectorate, dating from 1903, were simply Queen Victoria stamps of India overprinted BRITISH SOMALILAND (even though by that time Edward VII was on the throne). Colonial issues continued until the establishment of the Somali Republic in 1960. This George VI coronation stamp, elegant as always, did duty for most of the colonies. It may be that, given the turmoil surrounding the abdication of Edward VIII, Great Britain decided to announce the new king's unexpected enthronement in gala style. Note the absence of any explanatory text.

SOUTH AFRICA

**This lovely peaceful scene belies
Apartheid's harsh and desperate cries.**

Unsurprisingly, black people figure very rarely on South African stamps up until the inauguration of Nelson Mandela in 1994; it was as if the majority of the country's population simply didn't exist. Today South Africa produces colourful, sophisticated stamps of thematic interest. But even in the bad old days some beautiful stamps were issued, notably the 1926 bilingual-pair pictorial set which includes this one, featuring the *Groot Schuur* ('Big Barn'), a fine example of early Afrikaner architecture, and home of Cecil Rhodes, Prime Minister of the Cape Colony (1890–96). Rhodes's belief in Anglo-Saxon supremacy led him to enact voting and property laws that became the bedrock of South African apartheid.

SOUTH AUSTRALIA

**The queen seems suffering on this stamp,
Like Florence N. without her lamp.**

Concerned that the image of Australia should be forever tainted with convictism, the entrepreneur Edward Gibbon Wakefield set about turning South Australia into a colony attractive to potential settlers. He devised a plan called 'systematic colonisation', whose basic premise was the sale of land at a fixed price and the introduction of capital and labour. The plan became, in Adelaide, virtually a city-state, since most of the surrounding area was extremely inhospitable to permanent settlement (this being the land of the Nullarbor Plain and Lake Eyre). The territory was not fully explored until the 1890s.

Stamp design, in common with that of most of the fledgling Australian states, was unimaginative.

SOUTH GEORGIA

**Icy waters, krill and plankton:
Not so common in Southampton.**

This remote Antarctic region issued its own stamps from 1963 until 1979, before becoming part of the South Georgia and South Sandwich Islands. Its population is tiny, mainly a handful of scientists and support personnel. Its stamps are a curious mixture of royalty-gazing and genuinely interesting issues devoted to flora and fauna. None match the beauty of its first set, issued in 1963; surrounding the Queen with krill and plankton was a first for philately.

SOUTH WEST AFRICA

**These lofty trees, bilingual pair,
Of human woes have seen their share.**

In the history of colonial Africa, South West Africa (Namibia) stands alone in terms of exploitation at the hands of Germany, the Boers and apartheid South Africa in turn. Britain had decided that the financial return on a sparsely inhabited desert region would be too meagre to justify expenditure on a colony; in fact, South West Africa turned out to have enormous mineral resources.

The genocide of the Herero people (1904–05) was the blackest episode in German colonial history. South Africa, exploiting Germany's defeat in WWI, expropriated the region, continuing the racial segregation measures established by the German administration. As Namibia, it was the last African country to gain independence, in 1990.

SOUTHERN RHODESIA

**A frightful cove, that Cecil Rhodes;
I wonder where he now abodes?**

SOUTHERN RHODESIA – 1890–1940 trumpets forth this anniversary stamp, adding CECIL JOHN RHODES – THE FOUNDER. Rhodes, co-founder of the De Beer diamond empire, was an immensely avaricious megalomaniac and profoundly racist to boot. Together with the British South Africa Company he founded Rhodesia. As the first prime minister of the Cape Colony, he passed the Franchise and Ballot Act in 1892, limiting the native vote through financial and educational qualifications, while The Glen Grey Act (1894) fostered segregation along racial lines. Southern Rhodesia's transformation into Zimbabwe brought more misery in the form of Ian Smith and Robert Mugabe.

SPAIN

**Spain. Rain/manly/(mainly?) plane
(Work in progress)**

Isabella II (1830—1904) ruled Spain from 1833 until 1868. Her uncle's refusal to recognise a female sovereign led to the Carlist wars. Her reign was peppered with intrigues, an unhappy marriage and happier love affairs, an assassination attempt, and a very silly war over guano waged against Ecuador, Bolivia, Peru and Chile (The Chincha Islands War). She was deposed in the 'Glorious Revolution' of 1868 and abdicated in 1870.

This dumpy 1860 portrait pays crude homage to the Penny Black. Contemporary stamp design in Spain is vibrant; the long-running tourist series is one of my personal favourites.

SPANISH GUINEA

**A Spanish guinea?
Rather tinny.**

Spanish Guinea is now known as Equatorial Guinea, a small box-shaped country in West Africa whose capital, Malabo, is on the island of Bioko. There was no European presence on the mainland until 1844, when the Spanish made a second attempt at occupation (the first having failed owing to yellow fever). Profiting from Spain's weakness at the end of the nineteenth century, France was able to confine mainland Spanish Guinea to its present limited extent. Independence was granted following a plebiscite in 1959. This little stamp, a depiction of a *nipa* house (*nipa* meaning 'thatched' in Yoruba), is sheer delight: the frame is arranged in such a way as to make us think we are looking at a picture.

STRAITS SETTLEMENTS

**'Because strait is the gate, and narrow the way'.
That's a tall order, if you are Malay.**

It gets complicated. The Straits Settlements was a British crown colony on the Strait of Malacca, comprising four trade centres: Penang, Singapore, Malacca and distant Labuan. Labuan, which became part of the Singapore Settlement in 1907, was incorporated into what is now Sabah in 1946; Singapore attained independence in 1965, and Penang and Malacca joined the Federation of Malaya in 1948, prior to becoming part of Malaysia in 1963.

And that was the end of the Straits Settlements.

SUDAN

**Sudan is now a land divided.
The war is over. It's been decided.**

Sudan is a country we associate with the breaking up of its constituent parts into northern and southern entities, as well as the half-mad General Gordon. Modern Sudanese issues are sober and well designed, but cannot compete with the early issues, when the country was under joint Anglo-Egyptian administration. These feature the famous 'Arab Postman', seated on a camel, and are accessible to all collectors' budgets. This beautiful 1951 stamp (the double circle in blue and black was something of an innovation for the time) features a member of the Hadendowa tribe, known for its support of the messianic figure of the Mahdi, Gordon's nemesis.

SURINAME

**Little galleon plies the main,
On its way to Suriname.**

The Dutch South American colonial empire consisted of (briefly) Brazil as well as Suriname, independent since 1975. Suriname fell into Dutch hands as a result of an exchange, being the price received for ceding New Amsterdam (now New York) to Britain. Suriname's initial wealth came from slave-worked plantations; later, aluminium exports gained in importance from 1916, thanks to US investment. Fine examples of Dutch colonial architecture are to be found in the capital, Paramaribo.

This charmingly naïve 1936 issue, redolent of the superlative design for a boys' comic, features the galleon *Johannes van Walbeeck*. Van Walbeeck was a Dutch navigator and cartographer.

SWAZILAND

**There's lots of sand
In Swaziland.**

Many African colonies changed their names on independence (thus Basutoland became Lesotho, Bechuanaland Botswana, and so on). Swaziland (now Eswatini) kept its name until 2018. The name Swazi is the anglicised name of an early king and nation builder, King Mswati II. In April 2018 King Mswati III announced that he was changing the official name of the country from the Kingdom of Swaziland to the Kingdom of Eswatini, thus making it the youngest country in the world.

There is an air of calm nonchalance about this lovely 1956 view of the Highveld; the Queen, unruffled, gazes on her realm, the weather is lovely, and Enid Blyton is dropping round for tea.

SWEDEN

**'Young man,' they said, 'Go east of Eden,
And there you'll find a land called Sweden.'**

Sweden is known to philatelists mainly on account of the *Tre skilling* colour error: somehow a not particularly beautiful stamp (Sweden's first) that should have been blue-green was printed on yellow paper, and since only one copy has ever been found, it commands a huge price whenever it comes on the market.

Swedish stamp design came into its own from the mid-1920s on, although it remained monochrome until 1955, and seemed reluctant to indulge in colour on a regular basis until the 1970s – in itself a sign of confidence in its own formidable graphic design ability. This 1891 issue dresses up a simple numeral in very fancy clothes.

SWITZERLAND

©Post CH AG

Res Publica Helvetiorum
Means 'Treat this country with decorum.'

This breathtakingly beautiful 1949 stamp, featuring a stylised Lake Lucerne and the Dam near Melide, is from a definitive set of 'Technology and Landscapes' designed by Karl Bickel (1886—1982). Bickel's greatest achievement was his life's work, the Paxmal Peace Monument near Walenstadt, on which he worked from 1924 to 1949.

Bickel takes great pains to fuse natural and manmade in this set. His stylised vision of a world of unlimited potential is stamp design at its best.

SYRIA

**What a stitch-up, Sykes-Picot –
Now a war zone, total no-go.**

The 1916 Sykes-Picot Agreement between Britain and France saw the beginning of a lengthy process by which the bones of the Ottoman carcass were picked dry. Much of the Middle East, including Syria, was sold down the Euphrates; there was never a question of consulting the opinion of local populations.

Early stamps are those of French-occupied Syria from 1919 to 1921, then for the mandated territory until independence in 1942, and also for the United Arab Republic (comprising Egypt and Syria) from 1958 to 1961. Modern issues are quite attractive if somewhat overcrowded. The progeny of this fine 1946 *cheval arabe* can be seen thundering along the rails of the Curragh and Goodwood every other week.

TAIWAN

**It is, it isn't part of China…
Let's glue it on to Carolina.**

The Stanley Gibbons catalogue treats Taiwan as a Chinese province; for what it's worth I give it a separate listing. As of 2020, eighteen countries, mostly in Latin America and Oceania, recognise Taiwan as a nation state.

Taiwan was part of the Japanese Empire from the end of the nineteenth century until the end of WWII. Japanese rule was generally considered to have been beneficial to the island, so much so that many Taiwanese fought alongside Japanese troops. The defeat of Chiang Kai-Shek at the hands of Mao led to the arrival of 1,500,000 Chinese refugees on the island.

If you *must* feature bananas on stamps, this is the way to do it.

TANGANYIKA

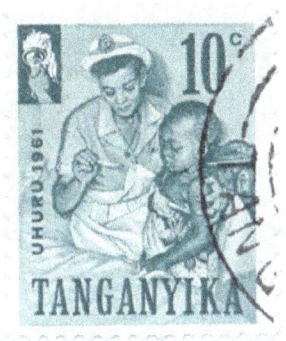

**First time I felt that needle
I hollered for the beadle.**

Formerly German East Africa, Tanganyika was under British mandate following WWI, attaining independence as Tanzania in 1961. Like other colonial powers, the Germans expanded their empire in the Great Lakes region in 1885 ostensibly to fight slavery and the slave trade; they did neither. Ugly incidents occurred, notably the Maji-Maji Rebellion in 1905, which was brutally repressed. William Boyd's novel about the WWI Anglo-German conflict in the region, *An Ice Cream War,* is well worth reading.

This 1961 stamp, one of the independence set, shows a reassuring medical scene flanked by the Uhuru Torch, the country's national symbol.

TANZANIA

**Dar-es-Salaam, tricky name;
Lovely fishes all the same.**

Formerly Tanganyika (q.v.), also incorporating Zanzibar (q.v.). The country's founding father, Julius Nyerere, stressed the importance of self-reliance: political freedom was useless if the country was to be enslaved by foreign investors, and people should work together for their mutual benefit in cooperative villages. Sadly, his views were rejected.

This 1967 stamp is actually a painting; few later issues can match its effective simplicity. A stylised form of the national coat of arms is visible in the top left-hand corner.

TASMANIA

**This little isle, oft quite forgot,
Hath devils fierce and wild begot.**

Named after the Dutch explorer and navigator Abel Janszoon Tasman, Tasmania was originally called Van Diemen's Land. Known as a penal colony, its early history was marked by the Cape Grim Massacre in 1828, part of the lengthy 'Black War' between colonists and the indigenous population. But Tasmania is also known for its stunning scenery, featured on this 1899 stamp depicting Lake Marion. This is the only Tasmanian pictorial set, sadly. The first Tasmanian stamp, issued in 1853, was inscribed VAN DIEMEN'S LAND, and featured a remarkably crude portrait of Queen Victoria.

THAILAND

**The King of Thailand said:
'Tis *my* land.'**

Formerly known as Siam, Thailand has never been colonised in recent times, a rare feat for an Asian country. A constitutional monarchy, it was profoundly compromised by Luang Phibunsongkhram's military dictatorship (1938–44), which promoted a pro-Japanese policy. Taking advantage of France's defeat in 1940, Phibunsongkhram ordered the invasion of parts of French Indo-China, and in 1942 Thailand declared war on Britain and the US. Thailand's standing with the West recovered quickly after the war, however, given its status as bastion against communism.

Thailand's colourful issues are frequently punctuated with portraits of the reigning monarch. This 1955 stamp was issued to commemorate the 400th birthday of King Naresuan (1555—1605).

THRACE

**This country has, by God's good grace,
Quite disappeared – without a thrace.**

The borders of Thrace have changed constantly throughout history. A map of Thrace in 386 BC shows it occupying much the same area as today's Bulgaria. About one fourth of Thrace lies in Turkey, about one tenth in Greece, and the remainder in Bulgaria itself.

An overprint usually means either 1) we are independent, or 2) we have been overrun. The only stamps issued for this never-to-be-country were Greek, Bulgarian and Turkish overprints, like the one shown here, a poorly executed Bulgarian stamp overprinted in French.

TOGO

**I came across a land called Togo
While leafing through my catalogo.**

Togo's colonial history is more complex than most: before the arrival of the Germans in 1884 it formed a buffer zone between the states of Asante and Dahomey, and its various ethnic groups lived in general isolation from each other. In 1884 it became part of the short-lived and brutal Togoland German Protectorate, which was occupied by British and French forces in 1914. In 1922 the League of Nations assigned Eastern Togoland to France and Western Togoland to Britain. In 1957 British Togoland was incorporated into the Gold Coast, and French Togoland became an autonomous republic within the French Union. Togo gained independence in 1960.

This pleasing 1968 stamp shows a simple drawing of a modern Togolese textile plant, contrasted with Van Gogh's *The Weaver at the Loom*.

TOLIMA

**The Granadine Confederation
Delayed the birth of a great nation.**

A state in the Granadine Confederation, now one of the departments of Colombia, Tolima is known for writers such as Arturo Camacho Ramíez and Martín Pomala, as well as seismic activity: the Armero Tragedy of 1985, in which the Nevado del Ruiz stratovolcano erupted, claimed 22,000 lives.

In this 1884 imperforate stamp we see the same old conservative patriarchal eagle common to other Granadine issues, but the rest of the stamp shows evidence of a creative mind.

TONGA

**Queen Salote, a monarch proud:
No booze or nicotine allowed.**

Tonga is a widely dispersed Pacific archipelago consisting of 170 islands, nicknamed 'The Friendly Islands' by Captain Cook. It became a British protectorate in 1900, ostensibly to discourage German advances in the region. Queen Salote (1900—1965), featured on this flamboyant 1920 stamp, was remarkable for her height; at 6'3" she was probably the tallest queen ever. She was also a keen writer of songs and love poems, which were published in 2004.

Tonga's most interesting stamps date from the 1960s and 1970s, coming in a variety of weird and wonderful sizes and shapes, a revolutionary idea at the time.

TRANSCAUCASIAN FEDERATION

**Belching chimneys, sooty fields:
Not so good for harvest yields.**

The short-lived Transcaucasian Federation of Armenia, Azerbaijan and Georgia was absorbed into the USSR in 1923. The Federation lasted just one month; it was never anything more than a pipe dream, given ethnic tensions between the three constituent countries. Faced with Turkish aggression, Georgia, followed by Azerbaijan and Armenia, declared independence. The Federation issued stamps in two designs: this grim one depicting Mount Ararat and belching chimneys, and the other (equally grim) depicting Mount Ararat, Elbruz and oil derricks. A few desultory berries and sundry squiggly bits make a cameo appearance. Better execution and, above all, better quality paper would have transformed the design.

TRANSKEI

**The white man's sop to independence
Was crooked in its very essence.**

Transkei was the first of the Bantustans in South Africa, a pretence on the part of the South African apartheid regime that a form of autonomy was being granted to black Africans. Upon the creation of a (nominally) independent Transkei in 1976, all black Africans with language ties to Transkei (whether or not they lived there) lost their South African citizenship and became citizens of the new 'country'. South Africa's cynical move was not rewarded by international recognition, although judging by the sophistication of its stamp designs it obviously hoped to pull the wool over many an eye.

TRANSVAAL

**Across the Vaal they rode, those settlers,
Wagons of elders and their betters.**

A British guarantee of internal self-government for the Boer population in Transvaal fell foul of the lure of gold, diamonds and other minerals discovered in the 1860s. The *Uitlanders*, or immigrant workers from Germany and Britain, found it difficult to accept the narrow cultural restrictions of Calvinism in the province, eventually provoking the Boer War. British annexation of the Transvaal as a Crown Colony occurred shortly afterwards.

A particularly poorly drawn eagle stands watch over an anchor (a reference to the Cape Colony, originally in Dutch hands), as well as a lion, a Boer warrior and a Trekker wagon.

TRAVANCORE

**How I deplore thee,
Travancore!**

Travancore was a former princely state in south-western India, now part of the state of Kerala. In 1741 it won the Battle of Colachel against the Dutch East India Company, resulting in the complete eclipse of Dutch power in the region. A treaty brought it under British protection in 1795. Travancore was known for its relatively high literacy rate and its progressive government. Following Indian independence, Travancore and Cochin (now Kochi) merged to form the state of Travancore-Cochin (q.v.), renamed Kerala in 1956.

None of its stamps inspire awe; this wretched 1911 effort is poorly designed and perforated, and printed on cheap paper. It features the flag of Travancore, a dextrally coiled silver conch shell.

TRAVANCORE-COCHIN

Travancore-Cochin, I'm sorry to say,
Was unable its mountain of debt to repay.

The merger of Travancore-Cochin lasted just seven years, from 1949 to 1956, when it was renamed Kerala. In that brief time it managed to get its philatelic act together: leaving aside the superfluous dowager aunt's earrings which flank the vignette in this 1950 stamp, we see a marked improvement in Travancore's contribution to philately, compared to the previous offering.

TRENGGANU

**In Trengganu did Ismaíl
A stately pleasure dome decreel.**

With Trengganu (now Terengganu) we bid farewell to the impressive canon of the thirteen Malay states. Under the terms of the Anglo-Siamese Treaty of 1909, power over Trengganu was transferred from Siam to Great Britain. Military force was used to supress an uprising in 1928.

We have seen that federal issues are used in tandem with separate issues for the individual states, generally featuring flora and fauna. This 1965 issue features a splendid *Paphiopedilum Niveum* flanked by Sultan Ismail (1907—1979), who gives the impression of being weary with affairs of state, even though his reign was described as 'a most eventful and glorious one'.

TRINIDAD

**Now, Trinidad
Ain't *all* that bad.**

Trinidad attracted little colonial interest until 1776, when the Spanish government encouraged Roman Catholics from the other Caribbean islands to settle there with their slaves, along with a promise of generous offers of land and tax incentives. By the time Britain seized the island in 1797, the slave-driven plantation economy was prospering. This 1896 stamp features Britannia waiting for the number 17 bus; a fairly orthodox design, were it not for the four six-pointed stars or hexagrams that frame it. The six-pointed star functions both as a talisman and a means of conjuring spirits and spiritual forces in diverse forms of occult magic.

What a vile postmark.

TRINIDAD & TOBAGO

**When these two joined up, no one thought
The British Empire overwrought.**

Tobago's development as a sugar colony began when it was ceded to Britain by France in 1763; by 1814, however, its importance as a sugar-exporting colony had already begun to wane. In 1889, with the island's economy in a shambles as a result of the collapse of its sugar industry, Tobago was amalgamated with Trinidad.

The 1938 set, like that of 1935, is one of the high points of British colonial stamp design. The portrait of the monarch, omitted in the earlier set, was restored for that of 1938, identical to its predecessor except for some proportional changes. The *Blue Basin* gets the full treatment: the foliage in the vignette itself is of Hergé-like quality, while the frame is one of the most exuberant ever seen in the British colonial stamp canon.

TRISTAN DA CUNHA

**The bloke they named this island after
Deserves to be hanged from a very high rafter.**

With a population of just 269, it is understandable that this remote island (the most remote inhabited island in the world) turns to postage stamps as a source of revenue. Discovered in 1506 by the Portuguese explorer Tristão da Cunha (whose cruel-looking portrait in a contemporary engraving may be a misrepresentation), it was evacuated in 1961 owing to volcanic activity, but the majority of the islanders returned in 1963.

Tristan's first stamps were 1952 St Helena overprints. This 1954 stamp, one of a set of fourteen, somehow lacks lustre.

TRUCIAL STATES

**Give me a word that rhymes with Trucial –
– Come on, guys, it's really crucial!**

The Trucial States were the forerunners of the United Arab Emirates (q.v.), and issued stamps from 1961 to 1963. Two treaties with Britain, the 'General Treaty of Peace' (1820) and the 'Perpetual Maritime Truce' (1853) gave the Trucial Coast its name.

The Trucial States produced just one set of stamps, in 1961, and got it right first time: this elegant dhow is positively Narnian, while the frame is a work of art, with its stylised ceremonial sash on a plain background. Note the no-nonsense country name in English and Arabic and the two medallions showing the stamp's value, polished to a blinding glitter.

TUNISIA

**Tunisian dates, the best of all,
From lofty trees inclined to fall.**

Tunisia became a French protectorate in 1881, curiously enough not by conquest, but by treaty. Unlike Algeria, the French did not confiscate land, convert mosques into churches, or change the official language. Long periods of Ottoman and French rule gave rise to a cosmopolitan culture.

All things considered Tunisia has to be a serious contender for best African stamp design. Its issues are colourful, confident and on the whole tend to avoid the overcrowding of many pan-Arabian stamps. This exuberant 1959 issue is wonderfully stylised.

TURKEY

**Turkish Delight, a boyhood treat,
Exotic, perfumed, good to eat.**

Turkey's struggle for independence coincided with that of Ireland. Greek forces advancing on Ankara in 1921 were defeated by Turkish forces under the leadership of Kemal Atatürk at the Battle of the River Sakarya, and were driven back to Izmir, which Turkey then seized, expelling the local Greek population.

This seems as good a place as any to mention Turkey's generosity towards Ireland: in 1847 Sultan Abdülmejdid, encouraged by his Irish physician, donated the enormous amount of £10,000 for famine relief in Ireland. However, since Queen Victoria had contributed only £2,000, he was prevailed upon to reduce the amount to £1,000.

TUVA

How can you improve on Tuva?

Tuva (or Tannu Tuva), formerly known as Northern Mongolia, was part of the Chinese empire from 1757 until 1911, when tsarist Russia took the country under its protection. In 1921 independence was proclaimed for the Tuva People's Republic, but in 1944 it was annexed by the Soviet Union and made an autonomous region within the USSR. In 1961 its status was raised to that of autonomous republic. In its short existence as an independent nation it issued several very attractive stamps, many in triangle or lozenge format, and mostly on the theme of the great outdoors, such as this striking 1936 hunting scene.

UGANDA

**Ripon Falls & Speke Memorial
Were (for a time) quite dictatorial.**

Originally unattractive to British settlers on account of what were thought to be its limited resources – before the discovery of copper, tungsten, cobalt, columbite-tantalite (coltan), gold, phosphate and iron ore – Uganda's colonial history began in 1890. Britain's tenure seems to have been mostly benign, and important infrastructure projects were undertaken during colonial rule. Uganda's earliest stamps, or 'cowries', dating from 1895, are simply typewritten squares, intended for use by missionaries. They are presumably easily forged; genuine copies fetch huge prices.

This 1962 stamp, elegant though it is, hardly does justice to the Ripon Falls.

UKRAINE

Ukraine, a land of Cossacks proud,
Tall Danube reeds and bitterns loud.

In common with schoolboys brought up in a western democracy, I learnt nothing about Eastern Europe, so I was unaware of Ukraine's complex history. In WWI, for instance, Austrian forces retreating from the Russians in Galicia executed thousands of Ukrainians for pro-Russian sympathies; in 1920-21 Ukraine lost one million lives to famine. As this book goes to press, the war in Ukraine has entered its 218th day.

Ukrainian stamps are colourful and confident, occasionally a little fussy. This one comes from a 2007 set of small paintings highlighting traditional objects.

UNITED ARAB EMIRATES

**Little lands all grouped together,
Talking (as one does) of weather.**

Originally the Trucial States (q.v.), The Emirates hugs the northern coast of the Arabian Peninsula. It consists of seven tiny statelets: Abu Dhabi (q.v.), Ajman (q.v.), Dubai (q.v.), Fujairah, Ras al Khaima, Sharjah and Umm al Quwain. External events such as the Gulf War (1990–91) and an ongoing territorial dispute with Iran have served to strengthen the Emirates' political cohesion, as have its colossal oil reserves. This view of Khor Fakkan, a resort in Sharjah, comes from the country's first issue, a series of views dated 1973. In the background can be seen the dramatic Hajar Mountains. Later issues are mostly well designed.

UNITED NATIONS

**Pen-pushers' den, beset by scandal,
Far too much for Trump to handle.**

On balance, the failures of the UN since its inception in 1948 (the Israeli Occupation, the genocides in Cambodia, Rwanda and Uganda, the Srebrenica Massacre) are to a certain extent offset by its successes: provision of food to ninety million people, assistance to thirty-four million refugees, electoral surveillance in fifty countries. The organisation's greatest failure though is inbuilt: its unwillingness or inability to dismantle the permanent Security Council, seriously compromising its power.

Dullest of the dull, this stamp.

UNITED STATES

**By rights this land was Cherokee or some such,
Not French or English, still less Dutch.**

Sadly, in my opinion the US contribution to philately is meagre: many of the early issues are unspeakably dull, and in fact we have to wait until the 1970s for the depressive pall to lift. More recent issues are a distinct improvement.

I rather like this 1968 prairie landscape issued to commemorate the centenary of Illinois' statehood, complete with Alabama postmark and serial number on the selvage (a technical term for edging).

UPPER SILESIA

**Divided down the middle,
A German-Polish riddle.**

Three languages adorn this elaborate stamp in which a dove of peace hovers over an agro-industrial landscape. Upper Silesia is now in the Polish province of Opolskie, one third of whose population is of German descent. After WWI, Upper Silesia was the scene of three uprisings having to do with whether the region should be part of Germany or Poland, which, given the area's industrial importance, was a burning question. As a result of the final division of Upper Silesia, the Opole region remained part of the German Reich until the end of WWII.

This stamp was issued in 1920, one year before the plebiscite that saw the area divided between Germany and Poland; a kind of philatelic wishful thinking.

URUGUAY

**A cheerful stamp marked *Montevideo*,
Ruled by a president, *Presidideo*.**

In common with other South American countries, early independence in Uruguay did not imply freedom; much of post-independence South America was controlled by unscrupulous caudillos who clung tenaciously to power. However, the vicious military regime that took power in Uruguay in the 1970s has been replaced by a progressive democracy.

The unspeakably dull issues of the nineteenth century have cast a pall over much Uruguayan stamp design, but recent issues are a marked improvement. The naïve charm of this very early 1859 stamp featuring a *Sol de Montevideo* is appealing; remarkably, the name of the country's capital, not the country itself, appears on the stamp.

UZBEKISTAN

**If only it were ruled by bees,
Uzbekistan would be Buzzbekistan.**

Uzbekistan first tasted independence following the collapse of the USSR, so there are no pre-Bolshevik issues. The country's record of human rights violations makes for grim reading (*vid.* Amnesty International's 2019 report), although the practice of using enforced child labour on its cotton plantations has been diminishing.

In terms of stamp design, Uzbekistan seems to have avoided the baneful influence of the USSR, and later issues in particular are quite attractive. This 1993 painting of a *Tulipa Kaufmanniana,* or water lily tulip, native to Central Asia, is one of a set of six flower stamps.

VANUATU

**New Hebrides it was of yore,
Now some the new name do deplore.**

Formerly the Anglo-French condominium of New Hebrides (q.v.), Vanuatu was declared independent in 1980. 'Following great disruption and depopulation in the nineteenth century, practically nothing remains of the cultures of northern and southern Vanuatu.' (*Encyclopedia Britannica*). In recent times the archipelago was devastated by Cyclone Pam.

Stamp-wise, Vanuatu is a cross between Australia and the Channel Islands; the most interesting stamps are those of a flora/fauna bent. This beautiful 2001 sand drawing is inspired by an ancient tradition recognised by UNESCO.

VATICAN CITY

**World's smallest state is steeped in history,
Though many things remain a mystery.**

Created in 1929, the Vatican is about the same size as the campus of my alma mater, Trinity College Dublin. The Vatican's library and art collection are among the wonders of the world. The Vatican Gardens cover about half of the country's area, but as far as I can make out no vegetables are grown. Indeed, almost everything in the Vatican must be imported.

    Stamps are an important source of revenue for the Vatican; they closely follow Italian design, with a higher input of saints and popes. This 1933 stamp, featuring the Vatican Gardens, is one of a pictorial set; its ornate frame and generally genteel aspect is redolent of dioramas sprinkled with rose water.

VENEZUELA

**This man, named Simón Bolívar,
Created South Americar.**

Venezuela suffered more than most in the South American wars of independence. Bolívar's loss of faith in the nations that he had helped create provoked him to complain that he had 'ploughed the sea'.

South America's early stamps, it pains me to say, are among the dullest in the world, and Venezuela is no exception. The worst offenders are usually the stuffed-shirt founding fathers portraits, which would probably dissuade any child from taking up stamp collecting. As for this stamp, I found the inscription *E.E.U.U.* puzzling – presumably *E.U.* stands for *Estados Unidos,* so why four initials? A Venezuelan friend kindly explained that in Spanish the initial is doubled if the plural form is used.

VICTORIA

**This stamp's so small it must be tricky
To lick it without getting sticky.**

The economic historian Noel Butlin suggests that the Aboriginal population of Victoria in 1788 could have been as great as 100,000, given the richness of the land. By 1850 that number had been reduced to around 3,500, thanks to the genocidal policies of the sinister paramilitary Native Police. Prosperity for the white population was assured by sheep and gold, although the latter quickly dried up. Self-government was granted in 1855.

An uglier collection of stamps it would be hard to find. Portraits of the young and not-so-young queen were issued concurrently; many of them are poorly drawn, and some of the designs are frankly repugnant. This tiny stamp is actually one of the better ones, though one wonders how the crevassed hands of burly sheep farmers could have manipulated it.

VIETNAM

**The intervening years eclipse
This nation state's apocalypse.**

Stamps of Vietnam mirror the historical development of the country following the declaration of independence from France in 1945: a democratic republic (1945–51); an independent state, comprising Annam & Tonkin (q.v.) and Cochin-China (q.v.), (1951–55); South Vietnam (1955–76); North Vietnam (1946–74) and, finally, the Socialist Republic of Vietnam.

This attractive postage due stamp was issued in 1952 for the independent state. War issues for North and South, when not occupied with war propaganda, were reasonably well designed. Although stamp design for the unified country has been mostly dull, post-2000 issues show signs of improvement.

WESTERN AUSTRALIA

**This swan, decked out in festive yellow,
Is really quite a splendid fellow.**

Western Australia occupies roughly one-third of the total area of the continent. Not until 1826 did Governor Ralph Darling of New South Wales, perturbed by reports of French and American incursions, dispatch a small party of soldiers and convicts to stake a claim in the region. As elsewhere in Australia, disregard of indigenous land rights triggered Aboriginal resistance in the Perth region, and was quelled in 1834 only after an intense and bloody confrontation known as the Pinjarra Massacre. As to its stamps, I don't know what philatelic fairy godmother was flying over Western Australia at the time of its first issues in 1854, but the fact remains that almost all of its stamps feature this elegant swan.

WÜRTTEMBERG

**This postmark dates from '62 –
That's long ago for me and you.**

The former German state of Württemberg was successively a county, a duchy, a kingdom and a republic before its partition after WWII. Its territory approximated to the central and eastern areas of present-day Baden-Württemberg. Thanks to its alliance with Napoleon, it doubled in size and was elevated to the status of a kingdom. At the time of this stamp's appearance (one of the more attractive issued by the individual German states) it was ruled by Wilhelm I (reigned 1816–64), known for his successful domestic policy. Note the FREIMARKE, not the modern German word for a stamp, *Briefmarke,* and the absence of both the monarch's portrait and the country name.

YEMEN

**The currency back then, *Bogache*,
Rhymes nicely with the word *Apache*.**

Poor beleaguered Yemen. Much of its present misery can be indirectly attributed to the carve-up of the country between the Ottomans in the north and the British in the south (Aden, q.v.). The north opted for a market economy, the south for Marxism. Economic meltdown led to the War of Secession in 1994, from which the North emerged victorious. Central government was challenged by the Houthis, an Islamic militant group, who captured the capital, Sana'a. A Saudi-led coalition of Arab states with logistical support provided by the US and Great Britain attacked the Houthis, killing thousands of civilians. Starvation and cholera have stalked the land ever since.

YUGOSLAVIA

**Marshal Tito's iron hand
Did its best to save this land.**

The Kingdom of the Serbs, Croats and Slovenes was established after WWI. Many who had agonised over the 'Balkan Question' in 1912–13 might reasonably have supposed that the issue had been put to bed. Events after Tito's death sadly proved them wrong.

Yugoslavia's stamps are almost uniformly dire; it was alone among the ex-communist nations of Europe not to have seen significant improvements in design. Had this something to do with a crisis of confidence brought about by the gradual disintegration of the federation? This lovely capercaillie, the largest member of the grouse family, adorns a 1958 set with game birds as its theme. The exception that proves the rule.

ZAIRE

**It has another name now, long and clumsy,
But *I* think Zaire's far more chumsy.**

The Democratic Republic of Congo or Congo (Kinshasa) (q.v.) gained independence from Belgium in 1960. While it is true to say that the Belgian colonial legacy in Congo was ruinous for the future development of the country, the DRC (Zaire, 1971–79) has been very unfortunate in its choice of rulers. In a way, the disastrous civil war that ended in 2003 was waiting to happen, and the simmering unrest in the eastern part of the country has never been fully resolved. Full democracy has never really flourished: Kabila's determination to stay in power in 2016 led to election after election being postponed, and even the dubious victory of Tshisekedi in 2019 was challenged, although unsuccessfully. As to the stamp, it really is the best of a very bad bunch.

ZAMBIA

**Lusaka Cathedral, a cheerful pile,
Built to last a good long while.**

Formerly Northern Rhodesia (q.v.), Zambia post-independence was comparatively prosperous, thanks to its being the world's third largest producer of copper. However, international sanctions imposed upon the illegal Ian Smith regime across the border in (Southern) Rhodesia also hurt Zambia. In the 1970s copper prices fluctuated and inflation increased. By the 1980s, poverty was rife; even the economic upturn of 2010 has recently been eroded.

Zambia's stamps are rather good. This bold design is one of a set of twelve issued to mark the introduction of decimal currency in 1968, shillings and pence becoming kwachas and ngwees.

ZANZIBAR

**This ocean-going dhow, now,
To sail needs naval know-how.***

Zanzibar, once a major hub of the slave trade, was an extremely rich sultanate. Large parts of Tanzania once belonged to it before it was expropriated by Britain and Germany in the late nineteenth century. The Zanzibari slave trader Tippu Tip retired to his clove plantations there in 1890, immensely rich, after a lifetime's service to the Sultan. The Anglo-Zanzibar War of 1896 lasted just thirty-eight minutes, with the British emerging as victors.

Zanzibar's stamps – especially those featuring sailing vessels – were lavishly produced and very handsome, like this one, issued in 1957.

*Try singing this couplet to the refrain of Justin Fletcher's 'Let's all do the Conga.' Works a treat.

ZIMBABWE

A proud and fascinating state;
This lion king has got a date.

Ian Smith's illegal White Man's dystopia, Rhodesia, eventually crumbled, and was renamed Zimbabwe (possible etymology 'houses of stones'). Robert Mugabe, its first prime minister, immediately set about redistributing land held by the white minority. His long reign was a catalogue of misrule and misfortune: he was eventually placed under house arrest and threatened with impeachment.

Zimbabwe's stamps are well-designed, and mercifully unencumbered with portraits of Mugabe. This 1980 stamp features a – lion. In case you were wondering, there is a helpful inscription to that effect in the bottom right-hand corner.

ZULULAND

**Alas! My little story's ended –
But then, least said is soonest mended.**

James Michener, in his gripping account of South African history entitled *The Covenant,* writes at length about the Zulu leader Shaka (reigned 1816–28), who paved the way for the emergence of the Zulus as a redoubtable military force by organising his armies on regimental lines. In their later fight with the British, the Zulus traded some of their land to the Boers in return for military aid. In 1897 British Zululand was incorporated into Natal; the last resistance to colonial rule petered out in 1906.

In this 1887 jubilee stamp the young queen's demure features are treated to an exuberant Art Nouveau design. Though not quite so young: the queen was sixty-eight years old at the time. A case of philatelic legerdemain.

Select Bibliography

Antunes, Catia, Gommans, Jos and contributors, *Exploring the Dutch Empire.* Bloomsbury Academic, London and New York, 2015

Biggs, Fiona, *A Pocket History of the Irish Famine.* Dublin, Gill Books, 2018

Brendon, Piers, *The Decline and Fall of the British Empire 1781–1997.* London, Vintage Books, 2008

Carmody, Pádraig, *The New Scramble for Africa.* Cambridge, Polity Press, Cambridge and Malden, 2011

Chasteen, John Charles, *A Concise History of Latin America.* London and New York, W.W. Norton & Company, 2016

Conklin, Alice, Fishman, Sarah, Zaretsky, Robert, *France and its Empire since 1870.* Oxford, Oxford University Press, 2015

Conrad, Sebastian, *German Colonialism: a Short History.* Cambridge, Cambridge University Press, 2012

Hannigan, Tim, *A Brief History of Indonesia.* Tokyo, Rutland (Vermont), Singapore, Tuttle Publishing, 2015

Harms, Robert, *Land of Tears: The Exploration and Exploitation of Equatorial Africa.* New York, Basic Books, 2019

Jerónimo, Miguel Bandeira, *The 'Civilising Mission' of Portuguese Colonialism, 1870–1930.* London, Palgrave Macmillan, 2015

Minawi, Mostafa, *The Ottoman Scramble for Africa.* Stanford, California, Stanford University Press, 2016

Pakenham, Thomas, *The Scramble for Africa.* London, Abacus, 1992

Pakenham, Valerie (editor), *Maria Edgeworth's Letters from Ireland.* Dublin, The Lilliput Press, 2018

Said, Edward W., *The Question of Palestine.* New York, Vintage Books, 1992

Citations from *Encylopedia Britannica*

Armenia
Contributors: Charles James Frank Dowsett, Aleksey Aleksandrovich Mints and others
Title: Armenia
Publisher: Encyclopedia Britannica
Date published: November 20, 2020
URL: https://www.britannica.com/place/Armenia

British East Africa
Contributors: The editors of Encyclopedia Britannica
Title: British East Africa
Publisher: Encyclopedia Britannica
Date published: Invalid date
URL: https://www.britannica.com/place/British East Africa

Ghana
Contributors: Oliver Davies, Donna J. Maier and others
Title: Ghana
Publisher: Encyclopedia Britannica, inc.
Date published: April 1, 2020
URL: https://www.britannica.com/place/Ghana

Guinea-Bissau
Contributors: René Pélissier, Rosemary Elizabeth Galli and others
Title: Guinea-Bissau
Publisher: Encyclopedia Britannica, inc.
Date published: September 9, 2020
URL: https://www.britannica.com/place/Guinea-Bissau

Japan
Contributors: Takeshi Toyoda, Gil Latz and others
Title: Japan
Publisher: Encyclopedia Britannica.
Date published: January 14, 2021
URL: https://www.britannica.com/place/Japan

Malaysia
Contributors: Craig A. Lockhard, Zakaria Bin Ahamad and others
Title: Malaysia
Publisher: Encyclopedia Britannica
Date published: January 14, 2021
URL: https://www.britannica.com/place/Malaysia

Nyasaland
Contributors: Kings Mbacazwa G. Phiri, Kenneth Ingham and others
Title: Malawi
Publisher: Encyclopedia Britannica
Date published: June 29, 2020
URL: https://www.britannica.com/place/Malawi

Portuguese Timor
Contributors: The editors of Encyclopedia Britannica
Title: East Timor
Publisher: Encyclopedia Britannica
Date published: November 21, 2019
URL: https://www.britannica.com/place/East-Timor

Rwanda
Contributors: René Lemarchand and Daniel Clay
Title: Rwanda
Publisher: Encyclopedia Britannica
Date published: February 20, 2020
URL: https://www.britannica.com/place/Rwanda

Singapore

Contributors: Thomas R. Leinbach, Annajane Kennard and others
Title: Singapore
Publisher: Encyclopedia Britannica
Date published: January 09, 2021
URL: https://www.britannica.com/place/Singapore

Vanuatu

Contributors: Sophie Foster and Ron Adams
Title: Vanuatu
Publisher: Encyclopedia Britannica
Date published: April 20, 2020
URL: https://www.britannica.com/place/Vanuatu

Copyright Templates

Abu Dhabi: {{PD-United Arab Emirates stamp}}
Aden: {{PD-UKGov}}
Afghanistan: {{PD-Afghanistan}}
Aitutaki: {{PD-NZ}}
Ajman: {{PD-United Arab Emirates stamp}}
Alaouites: {{PD-France-exempt}}
Albania: {{PD-Albania-exempt}}
Alexandretta: {{PD-France-exempt}}
Alexandria: {{PD-France-exempt}}
Algeria: {{PD-Algeria}}
Allenstein: {{PD-old}}
Alsace: {{PD-old}}
Alwar: {{PD-Alwar}}
Andorra: {{PD-Andorra}}
Angola: {{PD-Angola}}
Angra: {{PD-Portugal}}
Anguilla: {{PD-UKGov}}
Anjouan: {{PD-France-exempt}}
Annam & Tonkin: {{PD-France-exempt}}
Antigua: {{PD-UKGov}}
Antioquia: {{PD-Colombia}}
Arbe: {{PD-old}}
Argentina: {{PD-AR-Anonymous}}
Armenia: {{PD-AM-exempt}}
Ascension: {{PD-UKGov}}
Australia: {{PD-Australia}}
Austria: {{„Briefmarke: ©Österreichise Post AG"}}
Austrian Territories acquired by Italy: {{„Briefmarke: ©Österreichise Post AG"}}
Austro-Hungarian Military Post: {{„Briefmarke: ©Österreichise Post AG"}}
Austro-Hungarian Post Offices in the Turkish Empire: {{„Briefmarke: ©Österreichise Post AG"}}
Azerbaijan: {{PD-AZ-exempt}}

My Little Book of Stamps

Azores: {{PD-Portugal}}
Baden: {{PD-old}}
Baghdad: {{PD-UKGov}}
Bahamas: {{PD-UKGov}}
Bahawalpur: {{PD-old}}
Bahrain: {{PD-Bahrain}}
Bamra: {{PD-old}}
Barbados: {{PD-UKGov}}
Basutoland: {{PD-UKGov}}
Batum: {{PD-UKGov}}
Bavaria: {{PD-old}}
Bechuanaland: {{PD-UKGov}}
Belarus: {{PD-BY-exempt}}
Belgian Congo: {{©bpost}}
Belgian Occupation of Germany: {{©bpost}}
Belgium: {{©bpost }}
Benin: {{PD-Benin}}
Bermuda: {{PD-UKGov}}
Bhopal: {{PD-old}}
Bhor: {{PD-old}}
Bhutan: {{PD-Bhutan}}
Biafra: {{PD-old}}
Bijawar: {{PD-old}}
Bohemia & Moravia: {{PD-old}}
Bolivia: {{PD-Bolivia}}
Bophuthatswana: {{PD-SAGov}}
Bosnia & Herzegovina: {{PD-old}}
Botswana: {{PD-Botswana}}
Boyacá: {{PD-Colombia}}
Brazil: {{PD-BrasilGov}}
British Antarctic Territory: {{PD-UKGov}}
British Commonwealth Occupation Force: {{PD-UKGov}}
British Forces in Egypt: {{PD-UKGov}}
British Guiana: {{PD-UKGov}}
British Honduras: {{PD-UKGov}}
British Indian Ocean Territory: {{PD-UKGov}}

British Levant {{PD-UKGov}}
British Occupation of Italian Colonies:
Middle East Forces {{PD-UKGov}}
British Post Offices in China: {{PD-UKGov}}
British Virgin Islands: {{PD-UKGov}}
Brunei: {{PD-Brunei}}
Bulgaria: {{PD-Bulgaria}}
Bundi: {{PD-old}}
Burkina Faso: {{PD-Burkina Faso}}
Burma: {{PD-Myanmar}}
Cameroon: {{PD-Cameroon}}
Canada: {{PD-Canada-stamp}}
Canton: {{PD-old}}
Cape Juby: {{PD-old}}
Cape of Good Hope: {{PD-UKGov}}
Cape Verde Islands: {{PD-Cape Verde Islands}}
Caroline Islands: {{PD-old}}
Cayman Islands: {{PD-UKGov}}
Central African Empire: {{PD-Central African Republic}}
Central African Republic: {{PD-Central African Republic}}
Central Lithuania: {{PD-old}}
Ceylon: {{PD-UKGov}}
Chad: {{PD-old}}
Chamba: {{PD-old}}
Charkhari: {{PD-old}}
Chile: {{PD-Chile}}
China: {{PD-anon-expired}}
Christmas Island: {{PD-Australia}}
Cilicia: {{PD-old}}
Ciskei: {{PD-SAGov}}
Cochin: {{PD-old}}
Cochin-China: {{PD-old}}
Cocos (Keeling) Islands: {{PD-Australia}}
Colombia: {{PD-Colombia}}
Confederate States of America: {{PD-USGov}}
Congo (Brazzaville): {{PD-Congo (Brazzaville)}}

Congo (Democratic Republic): {{PD-Congo (Kinshasa)}}
Cook Islands: {{PD-NZ}}
Costa Rica: {{PD-Costa Rica}}
Crete: {{PD-old}}
Croatia: {{PD-Croatia}}
Cuba (1899, US Administration): {{PD-USGov}}
Cundinamarca: {{PD-Colombia}}
Curaçao: {{PD-Netherlands}}
Cyprus: {{PD-UKGov}}
Czechoslovak Army in Siberia: {{PD-old}}
Czechoslovakia: {{PD-old}}
Dahomey: {{PD-old}}
Danish West Indies: {{PD-Denmark}}
Danzig: {{PD-old}}
Dedeagatz: {{PD-old}}
Denmark: {{PD-Denmark}}
Dhar: {{PD-old}}
Diego-Suarez: {{PD-old}}
Djibouti: {{PD-old}}
Djibouti Republic: {{PD-Djibouti Republic}}
Dominica: {{PD-UKGov}}
Dominican Republic: {{PD-Dominican Republic}}
Dubai: {{PD-United Arab Emirates stamp}}
Ecuador: {{PD-Ecuador}}
Egypt: {{PD-Egypt}}
El Salvador: {{PD-El Salvador}}
Estonia: {{PD-Estonia}}
Ethiopia: {{PD-Ethiopia}}
Falkland Islands: {{PD-UKGov}}
Falkland Islands Dependencies: {{PD-UKGov}}
Faroe Islands: {{PD-Faroe stamps}}
Federated Malay States: {{PD-UKGov}}
Fernando Póo: {{PD-old}}
Fiji: {{PD-UKGov}}
Finland: {{PD-FinlandStamp}}
Fiume: {{PD-old}}

France: {{PD-old}}
French Post Offices in China: {{PD-old}}
French Post Offices in Morocco: {{PD-old}}
French Post offices in the Turkish Empire: {{PD-old}}
French Somali Coast: {{PD-old}}
Gabon: {{PD-Gabon}}
Gambia: {{PD-UKGov}}
Georgia: {{PD-GE-exempt}}
German East Africa: {{PD-old}}
German Occupation of Belgium: {{PD-old}}
German Occupation of Lorraine: {{PD-old}}
German Occupation of Poland: {{PD-old}}
German Post Offices in China: {{PD-old}}
German Post offices in Morocco: {{PD-old}}
German Post Offices in the Turkish Empire: {{PD-old}}
German South West Africa: {{PD-old}}
Germany

Reich: {{PD-old}}
Weimar Republic): {{PD-old}}
Third Reich: {{PD-old}}
Allied Occupation: {{PD-old}}
DDR: {{PD-old}}
Ghana: {{PD-Ghana}}
Gibraltar: {{PD-UKGov}}
Gilbert & Ellice Islands: {{PD-UKGov}}
Gilbert Islands: {{PD-Kiribati}}
Gold Coast: {{PD-UKGov}}
Great Britain: {{PD-UKGov}}
Greece: {{PD-old}}
Greenland: {{PD-Greenland}}
Grenada: {{PD-UKGov}}
Guatemala: {{PD-Guatemala}}
Guernsey: {{PD-Guernsey}}
Alderney: {{PD-Alderney}}
Guinea: {{PD-Guinea}}
Guinea-Bissau: {{PD-Guinea-Bissau}}

Guyana: {{PD-Guyana}}
Gwalior: {{PD-old}}
Haiti: {{PD-old}}
Hatay: {{PD-Turkey}}
Hawaii: {{PD-old}}
Honduras: {{PD-Honduras}}
Hong Kong: {{PD-UKGov}}
Hyderabad: {{PD-old}}
Iceland: {{PD-Iceland}}
India: {{PD-India}}
Indonesia: {{PD-IDGov}}
Indore: {{PD-old}}
Iran: {{PD-Iran}}
Iraq: {{PD-Iraq}}
Ireland: {{PD-IrishGov}}
Isle of Man: {{PD-Isle of Man}}
Ivory Coast: {{PD-old}}
Jaipur: {{PD-old}}
Jamaica: {{PD-UKGov}}
Japan: {{PD-Japan}}
Jersey: {{PD-Jersey}}
Jind: {{PD-old}}
Johore: {{PD-UKGov}}
Jordan: {{PD-Jordan}}
Katanga: {{PD-Congo}}
Kazakhstan: {{PD-KZ-exempt}}
Kedah: {{PD-UKGov}}
Kelantan: {{PD-UKGov}}
Kenya: {{PD-UKGov}}
Kenya, Uganda & Tanganyika: {{PD-UKGov}}
Kiautschou: {{PD-old}}
Kiribati: {{PD-Kiribati}}
Korea: {{PD-South Korea}}
Kuwait: {{PD-Kuwait}}
Kyrgyzstan: {{PD-KG-exempt}}
Laos: {{PD-Laos}}

Latvia: {{PD-LV-exempt}}
Lebanon: {{PD-Lebanon}}
Leeward Islands: {{PD-UKGov}}
Lesotho: {{PD-Lesotho}}
Liberia: {{PD-Liberia}}
Libya: {{PD-Libya}}
Liechtenstein: {{„©Philatelie Liechtenstein"}}
Lithuania: {{PD-LT-exempt}}
Lourenço Marques: {{PD-Portugal}}
Luxembourg: {{PD-Luxembourg}}
Macao: {{PD-Portugal}}
Madagascar: {{PD-France}}
Madeira: {{PD-Portugal}}
Malacca: {{PD-UKGov}}
Malagasy Republic: {{PD-Madagascar}}
Malayan Federation: {{PD-Malaysia}}
Malaysia: {{PD-Malaysia}}
Maldives: {{PD-Maldives}}
Mali: {{PD-Mali}}
Malta: {{PD-Malta}}
Manchuko: {{PD-Manchuko-stamps}}
Marshall Islands: {{PD-Marshall Islands}}
Martinique: {{PD-old}}
Mauritania: {{PD-old}}
Mauritius: {{PD-Mauritius}}
Memel: {{PD-old}}
Mexico: {{PD-Mexico}}
Moldova: {{PD-MD-exempt}}
Monaco: {{PD-Monaco}}
Mongolia: {{PD-Mongolia}}
Montenegro: {{PD-MNEGov}}
Montserrat: {{PD-UKGov}}
Morocco Agencies: {{PD-UKGov}}
Morocco: {{PD-Morocco}}
Mozambique: {{PD-Portugal}}
Mozambique Company: {{PD-Portugal}}

Muscat and Oman: {{PD-Oman}}
Nabha: {{PD-UKGov}}
Natal: {{PD-UKGov}}
Nauru: {{PD-UKGov}}
Negri Sembilan: {{PD-UKGov}}
Nepal: {{PD-Nepal}}
Netherlands: {{PD-Netherlands}}
Netherlands Antilles: {{PD-Netherlands}}
Netherlands Indies: {{PD-Netherlands}}
Nevis: {{PD-Nevis}}
New Caledonia: {{PD-old}}
Newfoundland: {{PD-UKGov}}
New Guinea: {{PD-UKGov}}
New Hebrides: {{PD-UKGov}}
New South Wales: {{PD-UKGov}}
New Zealand: {{PD-NZ}}
Nicaragua: {{PD-Nicaragua}}
Niger: {{PD-Niger}}
Niger Coast Protectorate: {{PD-UKGov}}
Nigeria: {{PD-Nigeria}}
Niue: {{PD-UKGov}}
Norfolk Island: {{PD-Australia}}
North Borneo: {{PD-UKGov}}
North German Confederation: {{PD-old}}
North Korea: {{PD-DPRKOld}}
Northern Nigeria: {{PD-UKGov}}
Northern Rhodesia: {{PD-UKGov}}
Norway: {{PD-Norway}}
Nyasaland Protectorate: {{PD-UKGov}}
Oldenburg: {{PD-old}}
Oman: {{PD-Oman}}
Orange Free State: {{PD-UKGov}}
Pahang: {{PD-UKGov}}
Pakistan: {{PD-Pakistan-stamp}}
Palestine: {{PD-UKGov}}
Panama: {{PD-Panama}}

Papua: {{PD-UKGov}}
Papua New Guinea: {{PD-Papua New Guinea}}
Paraguay: {{PD-Paraguay-stamp}}
Patiala: {{PD-old}}
Penang: {{PD-UKGov}}
Perak: {{PD-UKGov}}
Peru: {{PD-Peru-organization}}
Philippines: {{PD-PhilippineGov}}
Pitcairn Islands: {{PD-UKGov}}
Poland: {{Polishsymbol}}
Portugal: {{PD-Portugal}}
Portuguese Guinea: {{PD-Portugal}}
Portuguese India: {{PD-Portugal}}
Portuguese Timor: {{PD-Portugal}}
Prussia: {{PD-old}}
Puerto Rico: {{PD-USGov}}
Qatar: {{PD-UKGov}}
Queensland: {{PD-UKGov}}
Réunion: {{PD-old}}
Rhodesia: {{PD-UKGov}}
Rhodesia and Nyasaland: {{PD-UKGov}}
Rio Muni: {{©-exempt Sociedad Estatal de Correos y Telégrafos}}
Romania: {{PD-RO-exempt}}
Ruanda-Urundi {{©bpost }}
Russia: {{PD-RU-exempt}}
Rwanda: {{PD-Rwanda}}
Saarland: {{PD-old}}
Sabah: {{PD-UKGov}}
St Christopher: {{PD-UKGov}}
St Helena: {{PD-UKGov}}
St Kitts-Nevis: {{PD-UKGov}}
St Lucia: {{PD-UKGov}}
St Vincent: {{PD-UKGov}}
Samoa: {{PD-UKGov}}
San Marino: {{PD-San Marino}}
Santander: {{PD-Colombia}}

São Tomé e Principe: {{PD-São Tomé e Principe}}
Sarawak: {{PD-UKGov}}
Saudi Arabia: {{PD-Saudi Arabia}}
Saxony: {{PD-old}}
Selangor: {{PD-UKGov}}
Senegal: {{PD-old}}
Serbia: {{PD-SerbiaGov}}
Seychelles: {{PD-UKGov}}
Sicily: {{PD-old}}
Sierra Leone: {{PD-UKGov}}
Singapore: {{PD-UKGov}}
Slovakia: {{PD-Slovakia}}
Slovenia: {{PD-Slovenia}}
Solomon Islands: {{PD-UKGov}}
Somalia: {{PD-Somalia}}
Somaliland Protectorate: {{PD-UKGov}}
South Africa: {{PD-SAGov}}
South Australia: {{PD-UKGov}}
South Georgia: {{PD-UKGov}}
South West Africa: {{PD-UKGov}}
Southern Rhodesia: {{PD-UKGov}}
Spain: {{PD-old}}
Spanish Guinea: {{PD-old}}
Straits Settlements: {{PD-UKGov}}
Sudan: {{PD-Sudan}}
Suriname: {{PD-Suriname}}
Swaziland: {{PD-UKGov}}
Sweden: {{PD-Sweden}}
Switzerland: {{©Post CH AG}}
Syria: {{PD-Syria}}
Taiwan: {{PD-Taiwan}}
Tanganyika: {{PD-UKGov}}
Tanzania: {{PD-Tanzania}}
Tasmania: {{PD-UKGov}}
Thailand: {{PD-Thai}}
Thrace: {{PD-old}}

Togo: {{PD-Togo}}
Tolima: {{PD-Colombia}}
Tonga: {{PD-Tonga}}
Transcaucasian Federation: {{PD-RU-exempt}}
Transkei: {{PD-SAGov}}
Transvaal: {{PD-UKGov}}
Travancore: {{PD-India}}
Travancore-Cochin: {{PD-India}}
Trengganu: {{PD-UKGov}}
Trinidad: {{PD-UKGov}}
Trinidad & Tobago: {{PD-UKGov}}
Tristan Da Cunha: {{PD-UKGov}}
Tunisia: {{PD-Tunisia}}
Turkey: {{PD-TR}}
Tuva: {{PD-RU-exempt}}
Uganda: {PD-Uganda}}
Ukraine: {PD-UA-exempt}}
United Arab Emirates: {{PD-United Arab Emirates stamp}}
United Nations: {{PD-United Nations}}
United States of America: {{PD-USGov}}
Upper Silesia: {{PD-old}}
Uruguay: {{PD-Uruguay}}
Uzbekistan: {{PD-UZ-exempt}}
Vanuatu: {{PD-Vanuatu}}
Vatican City: {{PD-Vatican City}}
Venezuela: {{PD-Venezuela}}
Victoria: {{PD-UKGov}}
Vietnam: {{PD-Vietnam}}
Western Australia: {{PD-UKGov}}
Württemberg: {{PD-old}}
Yemen: {{PD-Yemen}}
Yugoslavia: {{PD-Yugoslavia}}
Zaire: {{PD-Congo (Kinshasa)}}
Zanzibar: {{PD-UKGov}}
Zimbabwe: {{PD-Zimbabwe}}
Zululand: {{PD-UKGov}}

Acknowledgments

My sincere thanks first and foremost to my sister, Fiona Biggs, who in addition to agreeing to offer professional editorial services has dispensed buckets of sororal advice. Buíochas mór, a deirfiúr, ní fhéadfainn é a dhéanamh gan tusa!

The Philatelic Medal of Congress and Purple Heart (Second Class) I award to my neighbour Eric Joly for his endless patience in formatting my stamps. My sincere thanks to my good friend Donal J. Byrne, whose comments were all the more valuable given that he doesn't collect stamps; to Andy Harris of the Italy and Colonies Study Circle (UK) for his invaluable advice about the Penny Post in Great Britain and the background to the introduction of the Penny Black; to Anthony Hickey of the Germany and Colonies Philatelic Society (UK) and Chris Hitchen of the France and Colonies Philatelic Society (UK) for their copyright advice; to Marisa Galitz of the Society of Czechoslovak Philately, Inc, for copyright advice; to Lane Smith for kindly permitting me to use his fine illustration featured on the Slovak stamp, and to Paper Heritage UK for helpful information about the Czechoslovak Army in Siberia.

For their words of encouragement and copyright advice, my thanks to Laetitia Biolley of the Universal Postal Union; Lucille Yap, Senior Curator of the Singapore Philatelic Museum; Peter De Fré, Manager Philatelic Program and Sales-Marketing, Bpost, (Belgium); Beata Ekler, Kierownik Wydziału Zarzadzania Produktami Filatelistycznymi Biuro Filatelistyrki, Central, Poczta Polska S.A. (Poland); Kurt Strässle, Kultur- und Partnermanagement, Post CH AG (Switzerland); Benjamin Heinke, Deutsche Post DHL Group, Legal Post AG (Germany); Karin Kolub, Filial- und Kundenbetreuung Philatelie, Österreichische Post AG (Austria); Caroline Ritter, Assistenz Leitung, Liechtensteinsiche Post AG (Liechtenstein) and Marta Herrero Blanco, Subdirección de Filatelia Correos (Grupo Sepi) (Spain).

Some postal administrations, sadly, were uncooperative when it came to enquiries concerning copyright law (which explains the puzzling absence of certain countries), and stringent copyright laws for countries such as France and Germany have meant I have not been able to include their modern issues.

A final word of thanks to my wife, Myriam Sosson, who must have wondered when this whole philatelo-literary episode would end, but who has supported me in so many ways tangible and intangible.

www.ingramcontent.com/pod-product-compliance
Lightning Source LLC
Chambersburg PA
CBHW051553230426
43668CB00013B/1832